MindStore
for Personal Development

Jack Black

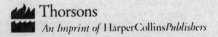
Thorsons
An Imprint of HarperCollins*Publishers*

For all MindStore Members who have participated on the courses over the years and whose fantastic stories and successes are a constant source of inspiration.

Thorsons
An Imprint of HarperCollins*Publishers*
77–85 Fulham Palace Road,
Hammersmith, London W6 8JB
1160 Battery Street,
San Francisco, California 94111–1213

Published by Thorsons 1996

10 9 8 7 6 5

A catalogue record for this book
is available from the British Library

ISBN 0 7225 3350 0

Printed and bound in Great Britain by
Caledonian International Book Manfacturing Ltd, Glasgow

Contents

Acknowledgements

Special thanks to my family, Norma, Anthony and Christopher, who continue to support my work and put up with the occasional limits on our time together.

As ever, there could be no MindStore without the wonderful team of people who work with tremendous enthusiasm behind the scenes to ensure that our simple yet empowering lessons can reach all who make contact.

Readers of *MindStore: The Ultimate Mental Fitness Programme* will be familiar with some of the material contained in this, my second book. In order to ensure that readers unfamiliar with the first book will be able to fully benefit from *MindStore for Personal Development*, the essential MindStore techniques have been reiterated herein.

Introduction

MindStore teaches you to have a positive attitude towards life, to manage your stress levels, to take control of your life, to enhance your creativity, to realize your full potential and to become the person you have always wanted to be.

Many of you reading this book will have been on one or more MindStore courses to help you in life or business. Others of you will have read my first book, *MindStore*, while some of you will be encountering MindStore for the first time with this book. Whichever applies to you, I hope that the techniques described in this book kick off a brand new way of life for you, as they have for the thousands of MindStore members in Britain and, increasingly, abroad.

Before I begin to describe the MindStore techniques, I would like to tell you how the concept of MindStore began and the fantastic differences it has made to my own life. And let me tell you right now, MindStore will have astonishing benefits for *your* life, too. As I always say about MindStore, *it only works*.

No doubt some of you are shaking your heads while reading this and feeling really sceptical about the claims I make for MindStore. That's OK, and I know exactly how you feel because I was sceptical too when I first discovered the field of personal development. In fact, when a colleague first offered to lend me a book on the subject I refused to read it and was deeply offended that he had dared even to suggest I might need it! But when I finally swallowed my pride and indignation, and started to read, everything fell into place. So please give this book a chance and read further before you make up your mind.

I am proud to be a Scotsman and proud to have lived in and near Glasgow all my life. For ten years, up until the late 1980s, I worked as a social worker in Easterhouse, one of the most underprivileged areas of Glasgow. Every day I was dealing with people who had lost hope because they felt they had no future, people who felt that life had dealt them a lousy hand and who were struggling against the odds. And, although I had gone into social work full of hope, ideals and a strong determination to change things, I knew that, in reality, I had been able to change nothing. We worked hard and tried our best, but it was like trying to bale out a ship using only a tea-strainer.

To make matters worse, I was losing hope. In fact, I was losing everything. I remember being in the pub one night with my colleagues after a sporting event I was involved with. One of the people there was the father of a very close friend of mine, so he came over to my table and we started talking. He said to me, 'I've noticed something about you, Jack, in recent times.' 'Really?' I said, 'what's that?' He told me how cynical I had become. 'What's happened to you, Jack?' he asked. I hotly denied that anything was wrong, even though I knew, deep down, that he was right. Actually,

I was sure of it. Almost every week I was convinced I had a life-threatening illness. I gave a whole new meaning to the term hypochondria. I practically had my own seat with my name on it in my doctor's waiting room, because I spent such a lot of time there. Every twinge, every ache and pain, every blemish sent panic messages shooting to my brain. Cancer, a heart attack, a brain tumour – you name it, I was sure I had it. If you have ever suffered from hypochondria, you will know what a controlling effect it can have on you. Then two of my colleagues died within weeks of each other, one from heart disease and the other from cancer, and my wife's mother died suddenly from a stroke. All three deaths left me shattered.

Money seemed to be slipping through my fingers, too. Balancing my budget was about as easy as balancing a stack of plates on the end of my nose, and I worried about every penny I spent. So I started a second career, organizing skiing trips, and although I was thankful to have the extra money, it meant I was regularly working an 80-hour week, with no time left for me or my family.

By now I had overcome my initial scepticism and started to read every personal development book I could get my hands on. The books by Napoleon Hill and Norman Vincent Peale had a really powerful effect on me. Having read them and absorbed the truths they contained, I could see how negative my life was and how full of stress, but I still couldn't turn it around. I could also see that my extended working week was not doing me any good, but I felt powerless to change anything. I felt I had lost all control over my life. I was no longer in the driving seat, I was not even a back seat driver, I was a passenger.

Finally, something had to give. My body decided that enough was enough and I collapsed. My doctor told me that

I had been given a powerful warning and had two choices – listen to that warning or ignore it and take the consequences.

From that moment on, everything changed. I realized that I had to learn to manage the stress in my life, and that was when the first seeds were sown of what grew into Mind-Store. As I developed the techniques that you will read about in this book, I got more and more excited because I knew they worked – I could see and experience them working in my own life. And they didn't just work in small ways, they worked in massive, fundamental, wonderful ways. This was something I could not keep to myself – I knew I had to spread the word.

It was not easy, and I spent hundreds of pounds on leaflets and mailings that were probably instantly filed in most people's wastepaper bins. I started to hold courses and only two people would turn up, one of whom would be a drunk. But I kept on because I had a vision of what Mind-Store could do. I *knew* it was going to work. All I had to do was keep that belief and be patient. Gradually, more people began to attend my courses, and what really thrilled me was that some of them came back for more. I was starting to see familiar faces in the audience, which was fantastic and truly empowering. Those early MindStore members began to give me really positive feedback. 'Hey, Jack,' they would say, 'you know, it works! I've been doing your techniques and I can't believe the results!' Of course, I already knew they worked, but I loved hearing about other people's experiences with the techniques, and I still do. When I give courses now, for anything from a small group of people to a couple of hundred to a couple of thousand, I still get a big thrill hearing how the MindStore techniques have made a dramatic difference to people's lives. Some of the stories bring a big lump to my throat because they are such fantastic examples of people discovering their full potential; I'll be describing a few of them in this book.

After a while I started to attract some big corporate clients who asked me to work with their staff. The list of companies I have worked for is as long as your arm, but let me drop a few names here to give you an idea of the wide range of organizations that encourage their employees to use the MindStore techniques. I am proud of them all and each one of them has a particular meaning for me, but one of the greatest satisfactions has been to work with the Metropolitan Police – I have taught officers to improve their performance, intuition and communication skills. I believe that is a real feather in MindStore's cap. I have also worked with some of the biggest financial companies in Britain, including Abbey National, NatWest, the Royal Bank of Scotland, and Standard Life. Some of the giants of industry who have sent their employees to me include Glaxo, Texaco Oil, Pitney Bowes, and Grant's Whisky. A particular thrill has been to work with some of Britain's greatest athletes, using the MindStore techniques to help them develop their determination to win – a determination that has been borne out by the fantastic results they have achieved. Among the athletes I have worked with are Liz McColgan, Glasgow Rangers football team (a difficult one for me, as a lifelong Celtic fan) and Gavin Hastings, among many others.

Let me explain a little more about the courses. At the time of writing, MindStore runs three main types of course: MindStore for Business teaches you how to set goals and make the most of your potential in business. (Although we do open-business courses, many of the courses are done in-house, either on their own or as part of a wider management programme that we call the MindStore Institute for Organizational Development.) MindStore for Life teaches you how to make the best of your life. The third type of course is called Discovery, and introduces children to the MindStore concept of making the most of their brains and developing their positivity and confidence, and also how to sleep better, learn and study better, solve problems and set goals. Incidentally, although many of the adults who come on the MindStore courses are sceptical, children absolutely love them and have no problems at all about what they are taught to do. That's because the creative side of their brains has not yet been trained to take a back seat to the logical side of their brains. That's something I'll be talking about in depth in Chapter 1, although all the tools and techniques in this book are designed to teach you to use both sides of your brain. Let me assure you that, when that happens, your abilities, performance and intuition are improved in phenomenal ways.

Whenever I begin a MindStore course, I tell the audience that the room we are in is like a departure lounge at an airport. Our flight is about to be called and we will fly off together into the sky. I am the pilot and the audience are the passengers, but it will be no ordinary flight, because each member of the audience will be flying off to a different destination. Well, the same idea applies to this book. I am your pilot and you are about to embark on what I trust will be a fantastic journey. The choice of destination is up to you, but I am truly going to teach you to fly.

The MindStore Approach to Life

I have shared the timeless wisdom contained in this book with thousands of people in Britain, and increasingly abroad, since MindStore first began in 1990. I hope you will be as energized and empowered by these MindStore techniques as I am and, as I always say, *they only work*. But first I am going to let you in on a secret. There is nothing new here. Everything contained in this book has existed since time began. The techniques are used in many different cultures in many different ways; what I have done is packaged them in a particular way – a way that I believe will help you to remember the techniques, enjoy using them and quickly start to see the results. After all, who wants to spend six months practising lots of techniques if nothing has changed at the end of that time? MindStore techniques start to bring results within days. But I don't want you to take my word for it, I want you to discover it for yourself!

Thoughts Are Things

As far as I am concerned, everything that happens in our lives is determined by our thoughts. *The quality of our thoughts determines the quality of our lives.* We have complete control over our thoughts – we can choose to think negatively or we can choose to think in a positive way. In fact, our thoughts are the *only* things we have complete control over. Every single word, every single thought, is processed by the brain. And that means, for most of us, that our brains are busy processing a whole collection of negative information every day.

Although the human brain is much more sophisticated than even the most complex computer, it is like a computer in some ways. For instance, both can only process the information they are given, so their performance depends on the quality of that information. Computer programmers have a wonderful phrase to describe this – GIGO, which means 'Garbage in, garbage out'. Yet most of us are putting rubbish into our brains (our bio-computers, as I like to call them), every day of our lives.

Of course it is one thing to know how important it is to have a positive attitude towards life. Adopting that positive attitude can be quite another matter, especially on days when your energy needs a boost or you feel challenged by events. Yet it takes just as much energy to feel unhappy as it does to feel positive. In fact, it may even take more energy. If you adopt the techniques in this book you will be amazed at the difference your change of attitude makes to the way you view your life and, as a consequence, the way other people view you.

Becoming More Positive

Being more positive starts with changing your vocabulary and finding positive alternatives to the negative words you have used in the past. I can always determine someone's mental attitude to life by listening to him speak, because his words reflect his thoughts. Have a think about the words you use every day. For instance, do you use the word 'forget'? The moment you say 'I've forgotten his address' or 'I've forgotten her name', you send your brain a very powerful message – one that says 'Stop searching the memory banks for that person's name or address, because it's gone forever.' You have just programmed yourself into 'forget mode'. An even more powerful message comes when you say to yourself, 'I know I'll forget to do so and so.' And you will, because you have just programmed your future in a negative way. It is what is called a self-fulfilling prophecy.

What you should do is programme yourself into 're-membering mode'. If you say 'I don't remember his address' or, even better, 'I'll remember her name in a minute,' you are telling your bio-computer, 'Start searching those memory banks, because the information we need is in there somewhere.' Your brain will process the word 'remember' and, sure enough, the desired information will pop into your head.

Take words like 'tired' or 'worn out'. We've all used them. We've all come in from a hard day at work or from battling round the shops, collapsed in a heap in a chair and said, 'I'm absolutely exhausted.' The moment you say that, your brain processes the thought and, sure enough, you start to feel even more exhausted than you were a minute ago. But if you say, 'I could do with more energy', your brain picks up on the word 'energy' and processes it.

Another word that sets up negative images in the brain is 'problem'. When you say you've got a problem it's like mentally staring at a brick wall. There is something insoluble about the word, and that is what your brain picks up on. However, if you change that word to 'challenge' or 'opportunity', you are telling your brain that you are facing a situation that will have a positive outcome, and that there is a solution. You are also mentally moving into the future, because you are looking ahead to the time when you will have the answer to the challenge. But if you call it a problem, you will remain stuck in the past, facing your insoluble difficulty forever.

As I write this chapter, the news headlines are full of the latest bout of flu sweeping the country, just in time for Christmas. It's the same almost every year and, amazingly enough, the predictions that the bout will turn into an epidemic often come true. Now, I think this says as much about brains as it does about viruses. I believe that the TV or radio tells us about the latest outbreak of flu and our brains start to process that information. Then, a couple of days later we start to feel peculiar, or to get a sore throat, or to develop whichever symptoms we have been told on the news to expect. 'Oh, no,' we say to ourselves, 'I think I'm getting the flu.' And what happens? Nine times out of ten, you *do* get the flu. You have programmed yourself to catch it. It's just the same as sitting opposite someone with a streaming cold when you are on a bus or train. You look at her belisha-beacon nose out of the corner of your eye, you hear her sniffing or sneezing, and you think, 'Oh, no, I just know I'm going to catch this person's cold.' Sure enough, you do.

Delete That Programme

The answer is simple: Don't get involved in forgetting things, don't get involved in moaning, and certainly don't get involved in thinking yourself ill. Whenever you hear yourself using a negative phrase or thinking a negative thought, there is a fantastic technique you can use to stop your brain processing the message. And it works! All you do is say, either mentally or out loud, 'Delete that programme,' then rephrase what you were saying in a more positive way. Next time you catch yourself saying, 'I feel lousy,' follow it up quickly with 'Delete that programme. I could feel better.' Try it. As I say about every MindStore technique, *it only works*.

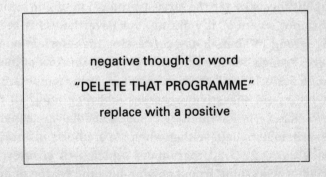

negative thought or word

"DELETE THAT PROGRAMME"

replace with a positive

Let me tell you right now that you will never be positive about the big things in life, the big challenges that will come your way, if you are not positive about the little ones. The sooner you start to choose a more positive vocabulary, the sooner your attitude towards life will change and, therefore, the sooner you will start to attract positive people, places and opportunities into your life.

Using Our Brains

All the examples I am going to give in this book are simple, because I find they're easiest to deal with and also easiest to describe. I have read many fantastic but complex books and research papers on the subjects contained in this book; really the principles are simple, and so easy to put into practice.

I believe that everyone has two levels of awareness – the conscious mind and the subconscious mind. We access the conscious mind simply by thinking – thoughts that range from basic questions such as, 'What shall I have for lunch?' to very complicated mathematical calculations and formulae, if that happens to be the way your mind works. However, we never have access to our subconscious mind, even though it forms by far the largest proportion of our brains. We are not aware of it working, but nevertheless it keeps going strong 24 hours a day, processing the information we receive through our five senses, regulating the flow of blood through our veins and arteries, monitoring our temperature, controlling our digestive processes and regulating all the other amazing, fantastic things that our bodies are capable of. Psychologists believe that when we are born our brains already carry 20,000 programmes which will ensure our survival – everything from knowing how to breathe to how to learn to walk. Unless there is a physical deformity, these programmes will be successful. We are, in short, programmed for success.

One of the things that really amazes me when I read about the human brain is how little of it we use. What would you say? Do you think we use 100 per cent? More like 75 per cent? Or 50 per cent? Only 40 per cent? Tony Buzan, the author and inventor of *Mind Maps*, has thought about this in some depth and, at a talk I heard him give in 1991, he said that if this were the 1970s he could say that we use about 20 per cent of our brains. It's not very much, is it? It must mean that we are missing out on so many things. But that's not the whole story. In his book *Make the Most of Your Mind*, he says he believes that now, in the 1990s, we use less than 1 per cent of our brains! This doesn't mean we are using less now than we did 20 years ago, just that as we understand more and more about the brain we realize that we are letting 99 per cent of this valuable and infinitely complex resource, the brain, go unused.

It's a staggering thought, isn't it? Especially when you consider how many magnificent things we have already achieved with our brains, particularly during the past hundred years. During that time, it seems as if our evolution has got faster and faster as we develop more and more astonishing inventions – cars, aeroplanes, movie cameras, television, computers, pioneering surgical procedures, space travel, and on and on.

Scared of Success

Yet even with all these accomplishments I fundamentally believe that the vast majority of us are frightened of success. We are frightened of living up to our unique potential, of being the person each one of us was born to be. Remember the school swot who always came top in exams and was the butt of everyone's jokes? Most of us looked at him or her and thought, 'I don't want to be like that, I want to be popular.' So, subconsciously, we sabotaged ourselves. We decided we preferred mediocrity to success. And we are still doing it. In fact, we are now living in a culture where some people consider it elitist to be clever, to be good at sport or to do well at school, because it makes the folk who are less talented feel bad. In the future our children may feel even more pressure not to stand out from the crowd by being successful.

By the way, when I talk about success I do not necessarily mean being one of the 400 top earners in the world, being the head of a company or being so beautiful or handsome that people swoon when they look at you. You can be a success as a parent, as a teacher, as a friend, as a painter, as a gardener – whatever you wish. Tapping into your brain's potential and being a success has nothing to do with academic achievements or being clever, either. Instead, it is about using your brain in a different way. A way that makes the most of your thinking processes and uses the brain's various functions to the full.

The Luggage of Life

Another challenge we all face is our limiting beliefs. By this I mean those ideas about ourselves that hold us back and stop us moving forward. Things like 'Oh, I can't do that' or 'I'm no good at expressing myself' or 'It's not going to work.' Ideas like these, as well as all our experiences in life, are part of what I call the luggage of life, all the thoughts and beliefs that we have accumulated over the years and that we carry with us wherever we go. For a few of us, the luggage of life is packed with positive ideas and fantastic experiences, but for the vast majority the baggage is weighed down with words like 'can't', 'won't', 'didn't' and perhaps even 'what's the point?'

Even though your luggage of life is full of disappointments, setbacks and challenging experiences, you may be reluctant to change the way you live your life because it is what you are used to. It has become your 'comfort zone', as many people call it. All of us have comfort zones about every aspect of our lives – as adults, as parents, as children, about being employed, about being unemployed, and so on. Have you ever met someone who is clearly not happy, and talked to him or her about life? Have you listened, and then made some common-sense suggestions about how things could change for the better, only to be given a long explanation of why none of your ideas is possible? This is what when a comfort zone is challenged. And if you picture a comfort zone as a tight belt around the waist, you will get an idea of how very restricting it can be.

There is a phrase that I fully agree with – 'Release the past with joy.' If you want to break out of your comfort zones and limiting beliefs, you need to study and understand the past experiences that formed those comfort zones, then release that past with joy and look to the future with positive expectations. I will teach you exactly how to do this in Chapter 3.

The Left and Right Hemispheres of the Brain

Until 1981, people working in the field of self-development believed that if they wanted to help people to take control of their lives, they had to teach them three things. The first was to give them techniques that would allow them to manage their personal energy. The second was to give them techniques that would ensure they adopted a positive attitude from that day forward. And the third was to give them techniques that would enable them to set goals for their lives.

Everyone thought these were the three golden rules, yet they did not seem to work. People went on the courses, listened to the seminars, read the books, got very excited about these ideas for an hour, a day, a week, a month – then lost interest and went back to square one. Nothing in their lives had changed. Obviously something was missing from the equation, because there were always a few people who were phenomenally successful. What was keeping them going? What made them so different from everyone else?

The answer came from two scientists: Professor Roger Sperry and Professor Robert Ornstein. They combined 25 years researching and studying the neo-cortex, which is the part of the brain just below the skull. They were looking at the brain's two hemispheres and they found that, contrary to accepted belief at the time, each hemisphere had its own functions. They found that the left side governs the logical, reasoning, analytical processes, and the right side rules the imaginative, creative, intuitive processes. When they heard this, the people working in self-development realized that the successful people they had been puzzling over *were* doing something different – they were using both sides of their brains. Everyone else tends to use only one side, usually the logical, left side.

Einstein was a classic example of someone who used both sides of his brain. Here was a man who was a renowned scientific genius and who won a Nobel Prize for his work on quantum theory in 1921; a man who was naturally gifted in left-brain activities. Yet he was also a concert-level violinist. If he had not made his name in science, he could easily have done so in music. What's more, one of his favourite sayings was 'Imagination is more important than knowledge' – hardly the words of a left-brain scientist. In fact, he discovered the theory of relativity by using his imagination – he half-closed his eyes one day while lying on a sunny hillside and looked at the sunbeams sparkling on his eyelashes. He decided to ride on one of these sunbeams and let his imagination take over. The results of this imaginary ride changed our whole understanding of science.

It was by looking at Einstein, and people like him, that researchers were able to realize that it is the people who use both hemispheres of their brain who succeed in life. In fact, they not only succeed, but accomplish achievements that set them head and shoulders above everyone else.

Once you know and accept this, it is very interesting to ponder the way most of us were brought up and educated. Remember when you first started school? You were taught your two-times table and things like that, which are logical, left-brain activities, but you were also given paper and crayons and paint and encouraged to develop your artistic, right-brain activities. Fantastic! However, once you started to grow up, the left-brain activities began to dominate. Science, history, geography, economics, mathematics and so on are all essential subjects for us to learn, and they are all left-brain ones. Most of us were taught principally left-brain, academic subjects, with right-brain topics such as music, art and dance relegated to a couple of hours a week or, worse still, considered only fit for pupils who did not make the grade academically. What our children need is to be taught a good balance of both right-brain and left-brain activities, so they can make the most of their both sides of their brains.

Tony Buzan has said that if we are to maximize our potential and use both our right and left brains, we have to imagine that we are standing on the wide band of matter within the brain (known as the corpus callosum) which connects the two hemispheres. That position enables us to access both hemispheres and, therefore, to improve vastly the quality of our performance. I am going to teach you precisely how to do this in Chapter 2.

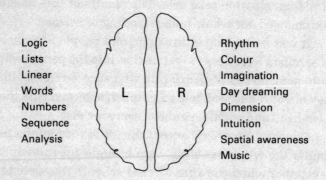

Logic	Rhythm
Lists	Colour
Linear	Imagination
Words	Day dreaming
Numbers	Dimension
Sequence	Intuition
Analysis	Spatial awareness
	Music

Managing Your Stress

For many people, stress makes them ill, makes them tense, strangles their sense of humour, makes them snappy and irritable, interferes with their digestive processes, and does a hundred and one other things, some of which you may well be experiencing for yourself. Even if you are not affected by stress, the odds are that you know someone who is. You may even know someone who has been killed by the effects of stress.

Life at the end of the twentieth century is responsible for a lot of these challenges. In Britain, especially, we are working longer and longer hours. Many of us feel as if we are stuck on a treadmill consisting of little more than going to work and paying the bills. Reading the newspaper or watching the television is likely to bring us face to face with more stress in the shape of bad news, depressing statistics, stories about death and murder and all the other misery taking place day after day. No wonder doctors' surgeries are crammed with patients suffering from stress-related ailments. And no wonder more doctors are experiencing them, too.

Indeed, only the other day I read that employees in Britain are starting to sue their employers over the amount of stress they claim to have suffered at work. Can you imagine what is going to happen if that continues? The courts will be full of people waiting to put their case and collect their settlement. And can you imagine how much stress the court cases themselves will generate?

The fact is that we all encounter stress every day of our lives; it is an inescapable part of life. The challenge is being able to deal with it. And that is where so many people have to resort to indigestion tablets, beta blockers, headache pills, days off work, too much alcohol, too many cigarettes and all the other things they use to help them cope.

Before we go any further, let me remind you that not all stress is bad for you. Good stress can save your life. Our bodies react to both forms of stress in the same way, because our hypothalamus, which triggers the body's reaction to stress, cannot tell the difference between a real threat and an imagined one.

Originally, stress was our early-warning system that something was wrong and that we needed to take action, fast. Whenever our Stone Age ancestors were confronted by a dangerous situation, such as coming face to face with a hungry sabre-tooth tiger or being threatened by an angry neighbour wielding a huge club, their nervous systems released the two stress chemicals adrenalin and noradrenalin into their bloodstream. This gave them the energy either to run away or to stand their ground and fight. It is known as the flight or fight response, and most of us experience it every day of our lives. It's fantastic if we need an instant burst of energy to take action, but it's not so great if we experience it over inappropriate events. That's when it becomes bad stress.

Let's say it's a beautifully sunny day and you're strolling along a quiet, leafy street. The birds are singing and it feels good to be alive. You see a friend on the other side of the road and wave, but she hasn't spotted you, so you decide to go and say hello. You step off the pavement and there's an ear-splitting shriek of burning rubber as the driver in an oncoming car stamps on his brakes in a desperate attempt not to run you over. What do you do? You hear the noise of the screaming tyres and your nervous system takes over. Instantly, your bloodstream is flooded with adrenalin and noradrenalin, your blood pressure increases and your heart beats faster. Your body needs more oxygen so you start to take quick, shallow breaths. Your muscles tense, you start to sweat and your digestive system shuts down, ready for you to take action – and, in less time than it takes to say it, you have jumped back on to the pavement with a leap that would not disgrace a world-class athlete. The stress response you have experienced has saved your life.

That was an example of good stress. But what about bad stress? You may encounter it almost every morning of your life. Imagine you are lying snugly in bed, all warm and cozy and fast asleep, when the alarm clock goes off. You are rudely jerked awake and, as your hand shoots out to switch off the alarm, your first thought is, 'Oh, no, it's Monday!' Your second thought is, 'Oh, no, I've got an early meeting with my boss and if I don't hurry I'll be late.' Your third thought is, 'Oh, no, it's raining, the car's being serviced and I'll have to catch the bus. I'm definitely going to be late. It's one of those days.' You clamber out of bed and shuffle off to the bathroom. On the way, you stub your toe on the toybox your daughter has left on the landing and which you have already asked her to move three times. And it gets worse. The postman brings a letter from the taxman which you dare not open, your bus is late, your boss is in a bad mood and, all the time, your body is producing more and more adrenalin to deal with this stress. The rest of the day goes well but you keep remembering that letter from the taxman and, each time you do, your brain responds by triggering the stress response again. That is because your brain can't think, it simply processes the information it is receiving from your mind – and your mind is thinking 'Help!'

Stress Overload

Now, our bodies are designed to be in perfect balance, and our brains are so finely tuned and sophisticated that they make our organs and glands automatically adjust their output of chemicals, hormones and so on whenever something is out of kilter in our system. So when your bloodstream becomes overloaded with adrenalin (because you are thinking about an imagined threat rather than using that adrenalin to deal with a real one), your body releases cortisol to counteract the adrenalin. Everything goes back to normal until, half an hour later, you again start to think about whatever is worrying you. Whoosh! Back comes the adrenalin, then back comes the cortisol to counter the adrenalin – and so it goes on until your body runs out of cortisol. Your brain is trying to keep your whole system in balance so it takes some of the cortisol in your skin – and you develop a nervous rash. Well, OK, you can live with the rash, but then your brain gets a message saying your skin has run out of cortisol. So it takes some cortisol from your muscles – and the back of your neck starts to tense up or your stomach goes into knots. Each time you worry, the whole process is repeated. When the muscles run out of cortisol, your body takes it from your joints and bones so, if this anxiety goes on for a long time or becomes a habit, you start to develop arthritis. And so it goes. In the end, you might develop heart disease, cancer, have a stroke or suffer from any of the other diseases so prevalent in our society. All through stress and worry.

No wonder we talk about worrying ourselves to death! And I should know – I used to worry all the time. I could have worried for Britain, I would have won a gold medal. Then I finally realized that my thoughts are the one thing I have absolute control over. We can all decide to think whatever we want. And that is the secret of your next ten minutes, your next half-hour, your tomorrow – your thoughts create your future.

Protecting Yourself from Negativity

We have all experienced times when we feel bombarded by someone's negativity. Maybe you are with someone who is having a right old moan about everything under the sun, maybe you have to deal with an envious colleague who is trying to needle you, or maybe you are stuck in a meeting that is becoming more acrimonious by the second. Instead of sitting there absorbing all the negativity and wishing you could escape, there is a simple technique that will allow you to participate fully in your surroundings while protecting yourself from the negativity. What you do is imagine yourself surrounded by a huge glass screen which looks just like an enormous jam jar. Its glassy surface allows positive energies to flow between you and other people, but it is impervious to negative energies, which simply ricochet off it and cannot affect you. Whenever I am in need of this shield, I hear the theme tune from *Thunderbirds* in my imagination and envision the glass screen dropping down over my head and enclosing me within its protective space. It works every time, and it is just as effective if you are on the telephone. Try it; you will never be affected by people's negative energies again.

Relax – It's Good for You

There is only one way to deal with bad stress, and that is to learn to relax. Sadly, many people find it very hard to relax because they do not know how to find the necessary time. They already have enough on their plates dealing with work challenges and their day-to-day lives, without finding more time to go to the gym or spend an hour lying in a flotation tank. That is why I developed the MindStore programme in the way I did. It teaches you to relax for at least three 10-minute intervals during the day (with more if you need them). Not many of us can find the time for one 30-minute session of relaxation a day, but all of us can snatch the odd 10 minutes now and then. In fact, it is better for you to have three short sessions of relaxation a day than one long one. And the benefits of each relaxation session last much longer than the 10 minutes you actually spend relaxing. The best times to do them are 1) when you wake up in the morning, 2) at some point during the day (many people find them most effective either before or after lunch) and 3) before you go to sleep at night. If you have time, you can also fit in a session at other times of the day, such as before you begin your evening.

When you relax, a number of important physiological changes take place in your body. The sympathetic nervous system, which controls the rate at which your heart beats, the rate at which you breathe, your blood pressure, your body temperature, your digestion and your muscles, slows down. As a result, your blood pressure drops, you breathe more slowly and the amount of acid in your stomach is reduced. Your brain starts to release serotonin, making you feel calm and better tempered.

Something else very important also happens in your brain when you relax, especially if you have your eyes closed

– your brain waves change. We know that there are four levels of awareness in terms of the brain's functioning, its electrical impulses and our states of mind. When we are wide awake, our brains send out beta waves. These are the waves that correspond to the logical processes controlled by the left hemisphere of the brain. When we are in a day-dreamy state, such as when we are sunbathing, our brain waves are in alpha, which is when the right hemisphere of the brain starts to operate. When we are in a light sleep, our brain waves switch to theta rhythms, during which our right brains are also working. When we are in a deep sleep, our brain waves are in delta rhythm; again, our right brains are active. (I will explain more about how to solve challenges and make the most of your time asleep using these rhythms in Chapter 5.)

BETA	WIDE AWAKE
ALPHA	DAY DREAM
THETA	LIGHT SLEEP
DELTA	DEEP SLEEP

Of these four states, the alpha waves are the strongest. They have a very powerful impact on the brain, one which I cannot stress enough. Almost all the MindStore techniques have been developed to work when your brain is in alpha mode, because that is when it is most receptive. Thinking in alpha and using it regularly will give you absolute and utter power in the way you shape any given moment of your day and your future. It will enable you to learn facts rapidly and remember them, enhance your communications, and give a phenomenal boost to your personal growth.

Quality Recovery Time

One vital part of learning to relax is something that I call Quality Recovery Time, or QRT. These are the times when you give yourself a breather from your daily activities and do something completely different and which you truly enjoy. It might be losing yourself in a good book, playing a round of golf, going for a swim, baking a cake – whatever makes you feel content and satisfied, and allows you to think about something other than your day-to-day affairs. For some people it might even mean giving themselves a lunch break for a change instead of working right through the day. Choosing to spend time in this way enables you to recharge your batteries, so that when you return to your daily activities or your desk you will do so with renewed energy and enthusiasm. You may also find that, while you have been thinking about something else, your subconscious has been working away in the background coming up with creative ideas and solutions to challenges.

Keep Smiling

One of my mottoes is 'keep smiling', not only because smiling immediately fills you with positive energy and makes you look and feel much more attractive than when you're looking grumpy, but because it has enormous benefits for your health.

As I have already explained, our brains are so finely tuned that they are able to process every piece of information they receive from our bodies. For example, your skin monitors the temperature of the air around you and your brain makes adjustments within your bloodstream whenever the air heats up or grows colder. Something else that is always being monitored by your brain is your facial expressions. Whenever you scowl or frown, your brain thinks you are facing that old sabre-toothed tiger again, and sends out a rush of stress hormones to enable you to fight or flee. Of course, you might be screwing up your forehead because you are sitting in bad light and cannot see properly unless you squint, but your brain does not know that. On the other hand, whenever you smile or laugh, your brain releases a flood of hormones, called endorphins, that are the body's natural tranquillizers. They are your own personal 'feel-good factor'. Have you ever noticed how much better you feel when you have had a good laugh? Even when you just smile? Can't you feel the tension just vanish and a lovely warm glow take its place? I believe that laughter is a very valuable part of life because it does us so much good. If you do not have enough laughter in your life, maybe you could incorporate it into your daily routine by spending a few minutes watching a favourite comedy video or reading a funny book.

In his fascinating book *Anatomy of an Illness*, Norman Cousins describes how he laughed his way back to health. He was suffering from an inflammatory disease which his doctors told him they were powerless to treat (not the most encouraging news your doctor can give you). Instead of surrendering to his illness, Norman Cousins decided that, as his doctors were unable to treat him, he would start his own course of treatment. He discharged himself from hospital and checked into a hotel, taking with him a collection of his favourite comedy videos and humorous books. He told his doctors that he was going to laugh himself better, and they were open-minded enough to agree to monitor his condition.

Every day he would spend a few hours watching films, reading books and having a really good laugh. Sure enough, he started to get better. What is more, his apparently incurable inflammatory condition also started to improve. So next time you feel in need of a laugh, follow Norman Cousins' example. Like everything else in this book, *it only works*.

Throughout the rest of this book I will give you tools and techniques to enable you to become a success in every area of your life. You will learn how to face the challenges in your life and emerge the winner.

2

The House on the Right Bank

The techniques described in this chapter are the basic MindStore exercises which will enable you to achieve deep states of relaxation and create a very special place inside your mind. This place is something I call the House on the Right Bank. It will eventually contain many rooms in which you will carry out a wide range of activities.

The House on the Right Bank, and the thinking you will be able to do while your brain is in alpha/theta state, are the most important parts of the MindStore technique. In fact, they will change your life. Positive words and attitudes are important too, of course, but it is learning to use your brain differently that will make the tremendous impact and change in your life, enabling you to achieve whatever it is you want.

I created the House on the Right Bank as something to focus on while relaxing, and also because it enables the right brain to work in tandem with the left, thus ensuring you make the best use of your thoughts. It took a long time and many challenges before I chose the House on the Right Bank as the ideal way to structure thoughts and enhance the ability to relax fully, both mentally and physically.

The house you will create in your imagination will have many rooms, each one of which will serve a particular function. Some are described in this chapter, others are mentioned later in the book. There is a room in which you can rid yourself of the negative energy and thoughts you have accumulated, and in which you can recharge your mental and physical batteries; there is a room in which you can boost your self-esteem; there is even a room in which you can prepare yourself for meetings and in which you will be able to improve your powers of concentration and recall. As you progress with the MindStore technique and become more familiar with it, I am sure that you will start to add other rooms to your own House on the Right Bank.

In this chapter I will describe how to achieve a deep state of relaxation, and how to create your House on the Right Bank, its Entrance Vestibule and Conditioning Gym, and its Central Hallway. As I explain each part of the technique I will discuss the importance of each new area of your house.

Relaxation Techniques

As I have already explained in Chapter 1, the right side of the brain switches on when we are in a relaxed state of alpha and theta brain waves. The relaxation exercise I am about to describe will help you to reach a state of deep relaxation, which will not only put your brain in alpha/theta mode (and therefore increase your creative thinking processes) but will also help you to combat the mental and physical stresses in your life.

Read through the relaxation exercise, then find a warm, comfortable room where you can practise the technique. If you wish, you can ask a friend to read the exercise aloud so you remember what to do, or you can read the exercise on to a tape and play that back. The ellipses (...) indicate where you should pause as you read it through out loud. Alternatively, you can use one of the MindStore pre-recorded tapes (*see* Further Information).

This exercise works best if you either lie down or sit in a chair; I would recommend that beginners do it in a seated position. This is because I believe that once you have learned what to do when seated, you will be able to practise the exercise anywhere – on a bus, on a train, before an important meeting, during the working day and even while standing in the supermarket check-out queue. If you try to do the exercise first time while lying down, you may drift off to sleep.

So sit up straight with both feet firmly on the floor – resist the urge to cross your legs or ankles. Sitting in a straight-backed chair may be better for this exercise than a comfortable, squashy armchair. Rest the palms of your hands on your lap, then close your eyes. Make sure you don't have anything in your lap or in your hands, because your body must be completely unencumbered for this exercise. If you wear glasses or contact lenses you may wish to remove them.

This first exercise gives you a taster of the basic approach. Each exercise is a stepping stone to the next. With each attempt you will improve your performance and develop a better understanding of the MindStore techniques.

EXERCISE ONE: LEARNING TO RELAX

Close your eyes and begin breathing slowly and regularly. You will now begin to focus your mind and body on relaxing into a healthy state of being. As different parts of your body are mentioned, concentrate on each one and focus your thinking on producing relaxation.

[Concentrate on your scalp ... Repeat mentally after me:]

I feel my scalp ... I am aware of my scalp ... my scalp is relaxing ... I feel my scalp relax ... my scalp is very relaxed ... My forehead is relaxing ... I feel my forehead relax ... my forehead is very relaxed ... Now my eyelids begin to relax ... I can feel them become limp, almost heavy ... my eyelids are relaxed ... This relaxation is now spreading around my eyes and beginning to relax the muscles of my face ... I feel my face relax – very, very relaxed now ... My mouth is relaxed ... I feel my mouth relax ... my tongue ... and now my throat begins to relax ... I feel my throat relax ... My head is completely relaxed, as my neck now feels the pleasant experience of relaxation flow slowly downwards from my shoulders ...

My shoulders are becoming very relaxed ... this warm feeling is getting deeper and deeper, my shoulders are very, very relaxed ... This deep relaxation is now flowing into my arms ... my arms are becoming very limp as the upper muscles of my arms now relax ... all the muscles of my arms are becoming limp and deeply relaxed, right down to my fingertips ...

My chest and upper back are now relaxing ... a warm glow of deep relaxation completely relaxes my chest ... my chest is very, very relaxed ... This healthy, relaxing glow continues to flow down into my abdomen and lower back ... The muscles of my stomach are very relaxed, very, very relaxed indeed ... My pelvic region now relaxes as the warm sensation continues to flow downwards, as I become more and more relaxed ...

The relaxation now flows into my thighs ... the powerful muscles of my thighs are now completely relaxed ... right to the bones ... I am so relaxed, just like the rest of my upper body ... it flows further into my knees ... my knees are now very, very relaxed ... The relaxation is now spreading into my calves, becoming ever more relaxed, very, very relaxed, and on down to my ankles ... They are now relaxed, so relaxed ... and now to my feet ... my toes ... the soles of my feet and heels ... completely, completely relaxed ... I enjoy the wonderful benefits of complete relaxation now ... When ready I am going to count from 1 to 7, and gradually adjust to come out of this healthy state of deep relaxation ...

1 ... 2 ... 3 ... 4 ... now, beyond the midpoint, when I open my eyes I will be wide awake and revitalized both physically and mentally ... 5, I begin to adjust my body ... 6, I prepare to open my eyes ... and 7, I open my eyes and am wide awake now, both physically and mentally alert.

The first time you practise this exercise, you will probably be surprised at how long it takes. Although it will feel as if only a few minutes have passed, when you look at your watch or clock you may find that it has taken a lot longer than you thought. Indeed, when I first do this exercise with the audiences on my courses, they are always taken aback when I tell them that the exercise has taken maybe 35 minutes, because they imagine it has taken 15 at the most. This proves that time does not exist when you are in alpha/theta state. In later exercises you will be able to take advantage of this fact in fascinating ways.

You may be wondering how you are going to be able to fit such a long exercise into your busy day. Well, let me assure you that you won't have this challenge, because after only a few practice sessions you will be able to dispense with this long procedure and become instantly relaxed when you close your eyes and breathe deeply. You will be able to achieve complete relaxation in only a couple of seconds, and become instantly relaxed during meetings, when travelling, when you grab a breather for five minutes or when confronted by challenges. I practise this technique at least three times every day and find it a wonderful way to combat stress and tiredness. Once you begin to practise it you will discover it makes a vast impact on your energy levels and will recharge your batteries in no time at all.

Using Your Imagination

Achieving a relaxed physical state is one of the cornerstones of the MindStore techniques because it allows your brain to switch into the alpha/theta rhythms which enable your creative, right-brain processes to start working and your logical, left-brain thoughts to quieten down. As Einstein said, **'imagination is more important than knowledge'**; later chapters of this book will teach you how to harness your imagination and intuition in spectacular ways.

You will probably have found that all the while you were concentrating on relaxing the different parts of your body, a little piece of your mind was distracting you. Random thoughts probably kept interrupting your concentration: 'What shall I have for lunch?' 'Have I fed the budgie this morning?' 'What shall I wear for that important meeting tomorrow?' I can assure you it's completely normal to be distracted like this. It happens to everyone who practises relaxation in this way, but let me also assure you that it is a challenge you can control. Each time you are distracted by a stray thought, acknowledge that thought and then *let it go*.

This is why it is so important to be able to relax your mind as well as your body – I am about to teach you how to do just that in Exercise Two. When your mind is in a relaxed state, your left-brain processes are no longer dominant and your right-brain activities come to the fore. With both sides of your brain now working, the quality of your ideas will improve dramatically. That is when you can start to uncover the full potential of your brain, and can start to develop your thinking processes in ways that will make you more creative, more inspired and better able to achieve the things you want from life.

So, to help you learn to control your thoughts I am going to ask you in Exercise Two to imagine you're in a place that you associate with feeling relaxed. I don't want to limit your imagination in any way, but you might like to choose a favourite holiday destination, a quiet spot in a beautiful garden, a fantastic sandy beach with palm trees and warm sunshine, the deck of a sailboat on a lovely, sunny day, a shady wood – whatever image makes you feel relaxed.

I am now going to ask you to engage all your senses while you imagine being in this relaxing place. If you were there right now, what would you smell? What would you hear? What would you taste? What would you feel with your hands and feet? What would you see? Not only does this technique enable you to control your thoughts because you are focusing on a definite scene in your imagination, it also helps your creative faculties to prepare. In other words, it serves to remind your brain of what will come next.

In order to help you improve your concentration and reach deeper levels of relaxation, it is a good idea at this point either to recite the alphabet backwards from Z to A, or to count down from 100 to 1. Because your brain can only process one conscious thought at a time, this will prevent other, unwelcome thoughts occupying your mind. This is worth doing to improve your concentration, but it is not vital to each practice session. Focusing your concentration in this way prepares your mind for entering your House on the Right Bank.

Once you are in this state of physical relaxation, which I call the physical foundation, I will ask you to imagine that you are standing on the bank of a river. You will be standing with your back to the river and facing a landscape of your choice. You can either picture a place you know, as you did with the previous exercise, or you can create a landscape of your own – it is up to you. I call it the landscape of abundance because it is abundant with your own ideas: you can create a beautiful, heather-filled glen, a tropical island, a lush garden, a fishing village – whatever you wish. You can include friendly animals, boats, trees, hills, mountains, lakes and all kinds of other features.

I call this part of your imaginary landscape the right bank of the river, because I want to associate it with the right brain. However, it does not have to be on the right-hand side of the river. All you will need to imagine every time you do the exercise is that you are standing with the river behind you and that beyond the river is the left bank, which is where you are when you are not doing the exercise. The left bank, of course, represents the left, logical side of your brain. So you will be looking into the landscape of your right brain, with all its rich imagery.

To help you connect with the landscape, I am going to ask you to imagine that you can feel the lush green grass beneath your feet, see the deep blue sky, and smell the fresh air. When you have stood with your back to the river for a few seconds, your imagination completely engaged in the scene, I will then ask you to walk into the landscape. As you do this, you will create the features that you want to see there – shrubs, trees, plants, flowers, animals, rocks, roads, pathways, statues – it's up to you.

As you walk into the landscape, you will not only be creating the features around you but also looking for the perfect location for the house that you are going to build there. When you see the perfect location, I will ask you to build a beautiful house there. This is your House on the Right Bank, the basis for the many exercises that you will find in the rest of this book. You will be able to develop all the wonderful tools that I describe in this book in your House on the Right Bank, so it is a very special place. Allow your creativity full reign in imagining what the house looks like – and remember that you need not worry about having to obtain planning permission, appeasing the neighbours or sticking to a budget. This is the house of your imagination, so build it in whichever way you wish. You can use a mixture of architectural styles if you want, build it from bricks, wood, glass, metal or any other material, make it a bungalow or several storeys high, choose something futuristic or utterly traditional. The only limitation I place on you is that the roof must be red. The rest is entirely up to you.

The final part of this exercise creates the entrance and the door, which face the river. You won't enter the house during this exercise, you will simply imagine the landscape and construct the house's exterior. Then you will come back to the river's edge and cross the river over to the left bank.

Now, before you do the exercise I would like to reassure you that many people doing it for the first time find it a challenge. Interestingly enough, the children who come on our MindStore Discovery courses (designed specifically for them) have a fantastic time using their imaginations to create wonderful landscapes and magnificent houses. They love every minute of it, because they use their imaginations every day, and all the MindStore techniques quickly become second nature to them. They can become second nature to you, too, even if your imagination is a wee bit more rusty than you would like. If you find it a struggle to make your imagination work, look through some magazines or travel brochures until you find a landscape that appeals to you, and browse through some glossy magazines on interior design until you find a house that you like. You can use these images for the following exercises until your imagination really gets going and your landscape and house evolve in the way you want.

As with Exercise One, you may wish to have a friend read the following out loud to you, or you may prefer to record it on a tape and play it back. Alternatively, you can read through the exercise and memorize it. Whichever option you choose, relax and feel good about it.

EXERCISE TWO: THE HOUSE ON THE RIGHT BANK
Once again, find a comfortable position in your chair, close your eyes and begin breathing in a regular and slow manner. You will now begin to focus your mind and body on relaxing into a healthy state of being. Again, as each part of your body is mentioned, concentrate on it and focus your thinking on producing relaxation.

Take a deep breath and relax ... take another deep breath and relax ... take a deep breath and relax ... My scalp is relaxed, I feel my scalp relaxed ... My forehead is relaxed, I feel my forehead relaxed ... My eyelids are relaxed, I feel my eyelids relaxed ... My face is relaxed, I feel my face relaxed ... My tongue is relaxed, I feel my tongue relaxed ... My jaw is relaxed, I feel my jaw relaxed ... My throat is relaxed, I feel my throat relaxed ...

My shoulders are relaxed, I feel my shoulders relaxed ... My arms and hands are relaxed, I feel my arms and hands relaxed ... My upper back is relaxed, I feel my upper back relaxed ... My chest is relaxed, I feel my chest relaxed ... My lower back is relaxed, I feel my lower back relaxed ...

My abdomen is relaxed, I feel my abdomen relaxed ... My hips are relaxed, I feel my hips relaxed ... My thighs are relaxed, I feel my thighs relaxed ... My knees are relaxed, I feel my knees relaxed ... My calves are relaxed, I feel my calves relaxed ... My ankles are relaxed, I feel my ankles relaxed ... My toes are relaxed, I feel my toes relaxed ... My soles are relaxed, I feel my soles relaxed ... My heels are relaxed, I feel my heels relaxed ...

Take a deep breath and relax ... I will now imagine that I am in a very special place of relaxation ... I am there ... I can see the scene all around me ... I can smell the scent in the air and I can hear all the wonderful sounds ... I will give myself a short period to enjoy this fully [pause for approx. 20 to 30 seconds] ...

Once again I take a deep breath and relax ... I will now imagine that I am standing on a river bank ... The river is behind me and I am facing a wonderful landscape ...

I can feel my feet on the lush green grass ... overhead the sky is blue and the air is fresh with the scent of the meadow ... I can hear the sounds of this wonderful land before me ...

Soon I will walk into the landscape in front of me, creating its scenery as I go in order to find the ideal location for my house ...

I now begin this beautiful journey, giving myself some time to create the landscape all around me ... [pause for approx. 1 minute] ...

I now focus my mind on the site where I will construct my House on the Right Bank ... First I create the walls, their height and features as I choose ... Now the windows ... the roof is red

... The entrance is welcoming and attractive to me ... I have now created the outer construction of my House on the Right Bank. I will use it to achieve whatever I desire for my life ...

I now leave the house and return to the river's edge ... I feel the lush green grass beneath my feet. Soon I will count from 1 to 7, and gradually adjust to come out of this healthy state of deep relaxation ...

1 ... 2 ... 3 ... 4 ... now, beyond the midpoint, when I open my eyes I will be wide awake and revitalized both physically and mentally ... 5, I begin to adjust my body ... 6, I prepare to open my eyes ... and 7, I open my eyes and am wide awake now, both physically and mentally alert.

Common Questions About the House on the Right Bank

Before we progress to the next exercise, which involves creating the Conditioning Gym in your House on the Right Bank, I should like to answer some of the questions that come up a lot on the MindStore courses.

Why Is the Roof Red?

I am often asked why the roof of the House on the Right Bank has got to be red. When I was putting the techniques together several years ago, I read a lot of research from China about how the human eye works. Sight is the only one of our five senses that is directly part of the brain – if you look at the back of the human eye you will see that the optic nerve goes right into the centre of the brain. At the back of the eye is a series of minute rods and cones that vibrate at different frequencies and allow us to perceive light. There are only three primary frequencies or colours – red, blue and green – similar to the colours used in television tubes and the primary electronic colours, but different from paint primaries of red, blue and yellow. With these rods and cones we are able to see every other colour under the sun. I decided that in the House on the Right Bank we would exercise these three frequencies – thus the green grass, blue sky, and the red roof. However, I also chose a red roof because most people who are challenged by creating visual images say that red is the colour they find least easy to imagine, so the red roof is a form of visual practice for all of us. By the way, many people have told me that they find it easier to see the red roof if they first walk through a field of bright red poppies in their imaginary landscape.

Challenges with Imagination

Some people have told me they find it extremely challenging to see the House on the Right Bank and the landscape. Maybe you are finding this true of you. Current understanding says our brains have three ways of thinking – visual, audio and kinaesthetic (*see* Chapter 3 for more about this). If your visual mode of thinking could do with some improvement, maybe you have fantastic audio abilities instead? Or perhaps your kinaesthetic abilities are strongest? Let me assure you that, even though I have been practising these MindStore techniques for over six years, I have never clearly seen my House on the Right Bank! When I close my eyes it's dark in here. My visual thinking could be a lot stronger, but these techniques still work like magic for me. Because even though I cannot see the house, I hear every single creak in that place! So remember that there are no rights or wrongs about which mode of thinking is strongest. The MindStore techniques were designed to exercise our audio, visual and kinaesthetic abilities, so don't worry.

A Changing Landscape

Another question I am frequently asked is whether the House on the Right Bank changes the more you visit it. You may well find when you start doing these exercises, especially if you have not used your imagination very much for years, that you're not very impressed with the landscape or the house you create. Maybe it looks boring, or perhaps you feel that your brain is refusing to co-operate. Well, keep practising and you will soon find that your House on the Right Bank begins to change and evolve. It might get bigger, it may have more interesting windows, or you could start to see architectural details that you had not noticed before. If that happens, give yourself a pat on the back. I have known some people who see five or six houses in one exercise and cannot choose which one they want. Well, that's fantastic! If this applies to you, it means that your right brain is starting to work. You will eventually settle down with a House on the Right Bank that you really like, even though you may occasionally decide to change some of the details. Every now and then I have a good spring clean in my house, I redecorate the rooms or change them around. Remember, there are no limitations here. It doesn't have to be a small, neat house with a square garden. It can be huge. It can be a space-age complex with the Hanging Gardens of Babylon outside. It's your imagination, so create whatever you want.

Crossing Over to the Left Bank

Many people use the counting technique at the end of the exercise not only to bring themselves out of the state of deep relaxation but to represent the steps they take away from the Right Bank and over to the Left. You can imagine hopping over some stepping stones or crossing a bridge to get to the Left Bank, or you could walk across, swim across, sail over on a boat, even fly on the back of a seagull. The choice is yours, so enjoy whatever you choose.

A Better Blood Supply

As you become more relaxed each time you visit the House on the Right Bank, you may find your body does strange things. Many people experience these strange happenings when they do the relaxation exercise for the first time. You may sometimes find that you become so relaxed that highly energized blood starts to flow through parts of your body which have not received such good stuff in quite a while, so you might start experiencing itches in odd places. Maybe the end of your nose will start to itch, or your earlobe, or your feet. Well, for goodness sake have a good scratch! Otherwise your concentration will not be as focused as it could be, because you will be continually aware of your itchy nose. Some people salivate a lot – I know I do – and have to swallow more than usual. You may find that your limbs feel different when you are completely relaxed – either heavier or lighter than normal. It may even feel as if your arms are floating in the air, in an odd position, or slightly numb. These are all signs that well-oxygenated blood is reaching parts of your body that have gone without for some time.

Stiff Necks

Finally, some people experience discomfort at the back of their neck at first. It can feel quite tight; this is because our heads are very heavy and, although our spines are designed to bear this weight with ease, for a variety of reasons we sometimes adopt postures that throw our neck, shoulder and back muscles out of balance. This causes tension in this area and so we take on new postures in an attempt to relax the muscles. Of course, these do not really relax the muscles at all.

You can be sure that any tension you feel in your neck and shoulders while you are doing these exercises will soon pass. As the exercises develop you will learn how to control your level of relaxation and therefore manage the levels of stress in your life. You will also be able to use all the techniques and tools that I describe to realize your potential and make vital changes in your life.

Creating the Entrance Vestibule and Conditioning Gym

The next exercise I am going to describe will take you inside your House on the Right Bank for the first time and enable you to create two very important areas in there – the Entrance Vestibule and the Conditioning Gym. Together these make up what I have named the Standard Entry Exercise. You will perform this exercise every time you enter your House on the Right Bank.

The Entrance Vestibule

When you open the front door and walk into your house for the first time, you will step straight into the Entrance Vestibule. This is an important area of the house because it will give you your first taste of the fantastic potential that is inside you, waiting to be released. Every room that you create in this house will enable you to achieve a particular aspect of your potential (and I hope that, like many of the people who have been on my MindStore courses, you will go on to create all kinds of rooms that I would never have thought of). I will explain more in a minute, but for now I want to talk about the appearance of the Entrance Vestibule.

Only you can decide what your Entrance Vestibule looks like. Only you can decide on the height of the ceiling, the colour of the walls, the colour and style of the floor coverings, the decorations, the paintings, the artefacts, the lighting and so on. Will it be lit by candles or enormous spotlights? Will it have marble pillars, old wooden beams or some fantastic futuristic decorations that only you can imagine? I urge you to use your right brain to create something absolutely wonderful, because if you build something boring in your mind, something that's dull and lifeless, then you won't want to go there. But if you really push yourself and decorate your Entrance Vestibule in the colours, shapes, beautiful artwork, incredibly expensive antiques or whatever it is you want there, you will get a real buzz every time you walk through it.

The choice of what to put in the Entrance Vestibule is entirely yours, but something that I do suggest is a symbol of your unique and marvellous potential. Something that will remind you, every time you see it, that you are a truly wonderful person with enormous potential. Many of the sports stars I have worked with have chosen their gold medals, caps or trophies. Artists might choose the painting or sculpture that they are most proud of. What do you choose?

While you are thinking this through, I will tell you what I have in my Entrance Vestibule. It is a three-dimensional hologram of my immediate family – Norma, myself and our two sons, Anthony and Christopher – looking healthy, happy and prosperous. Every time I see it, on my way in and out of the House on the Right Bank, it fires me with the energy and enthusiasm I need to travel around the country – and, in-creasingly, around the world – teaching MindStore courses and running the various areas of MindStore. That image gives me my impetus.

You may already have a suitable image in mind, or you may be mentally sorting through a variety of ideas but still not be entirely satisfied with any of them. That's fine. Wait until you enter the Entrance Vestibule in the following exer-cise and see if any symbol has appeared there. If it hasn't, then trust that an appropriate image will come to you soon-er or later.

The Conditioning Gym

OK, let's move on. In Exercise Three you will walk through the Entrance Vestibule, look at the symbol of your potential (if you have chosen one) and then walk into the Conditioning Gym that leads off the Entrance Vestibule. The gym is the first real room that you will create in your house. It is where you will prepare yourself for using the rest of the rooms in the house, and also prepare yourself for enjoying and getting the most out of your life. It is a vital part of the House on the Right Bank because it contains two important tools that will help you to boost your personal energy whenever you need to: a Shower, and an Energizing Beam.

We have all had days when we feel listless and have to drag ourselves around, days when even the simplest things seem to be too much trouble or when nothing goes as well as it might. There are also those days when we start off full of promise, full of hope, but feel absolutely crushed and dispir-ited by someone's caustic remark or negative statement. We get through the day but have no energy left for our friends and family in the evening. I am sure we have all experienced the feeling of longing to go home and curl up in front of the television, but then remember we have made plans to go out. It's very tempting to give into that feeling and cancel our social arrangements, and that is such a shame because it interferes with our enjoyment of life. It may also mean that we miss out on opportunities and advantages.

Something else happens, too, at the end of those tiring days. You come home to your family, or you get on the phone to a friend, and they ask you how your day went. And what do you do? You tell them, in graphic detail, how terrible it was, who said what, how angry or bitter you feel, what happened on the train on the way home, how you are dreading going to work tomorrow, or whatever is upsetting you. And whoever you are talking to will probably do the same to you. The result is two people who are now swamped by negativity. I used to do all this when I was a social worker. I would come home every night to Norma, who had her own demanding job as a teacher, and she would ask me how my day had gone. And I would spill negativity all over her. Then she would tell me how her day had gone, and so it would go on. We had nothing left to give each other in the evenings.

That is why I developed the two tools that you will create in your Conditioning Gym. The first is the fantastically powerful Shower. Water is a universal symbol for cleansing, so I realized that the first thing you need to do when you enter the Conditioning Gym is wash off all the negativity, disappointments and challenging emotions that the day has presented you with. Knowing that the brain processes thoughts with great effectiveness when they are in alpha/theta, I realized that this Shower would have really powerful results. What's more, I knew that, as with all the other MindStore techniques, the more you used the Shower, the more effective it would become.

When you come to create your own Shower in the Conditioning Gym, you can either imagine one of those tiny devices you find in some hotels and guest houses – the sort that make you feel as if you are standing under a watering can – or you can create something absolutely fantastic. My Shower has got marble pillars, fantastic flooring and a big cliff edge. At the top of the cliff is a big, rustic gate. When I press a button I hear the gate being slowly winched up, and then I am deluged by the most wonderful waterfall. Torrents of warm spring water cascade over me, running through my hair, down over every inch of my body. I tell myself that the water is draining away all my mental fatigue. And that is exactly what happens.

As well as lovely, fresh, spring water, there is also warm, radiant sunlight in this Shower. I decided to introduce sunlight so it would pierce into your brain and clear out any nagging little doubts or self-limiting beliefs, or any of the negative emotions we are so good at, such as pettiness, anger, greed, envy and fear.

When you step out of the Shower, you're instantly dry (there is no need for any towels in this Conditioning Gym) and fresh, with a positive expectation and a positive attitude, ready to make the most of the other techniques and tools you will find in the House on the Right Bank.

I strongly urge you to use this Shower every time you enter your House on the Right Bank, because what you don't want to do is enter this very powerful house that exists deep in your mind and reinforce all the negativity that you have collected during your day. You want to get rid of it, not build on it.

The other important tool that you will create in your Conditioning Gym is something that will instantly recharge your physical and mental batteries and fill you with abundant energy. I call it the Energizing Beam, and many of the people who come on the MindStore courses have told me of the remarkable results they have achieved when they use it. You will imagine that the Energizing Beam is mounted on a platform, and that whenever you stand on it you will be recharged with vibrant energy from head to toe.

After you have stepped out of the Shower, you walk over to the Energizing Beam and stand on it. Press a switch and imagine that vibrations full of health and energy are being pumped through your whole body, rising up from your feet and coursing through you until they reach your brain. You are now charged with energy.

The Energizing Beam will give you a fresh burst of abundant energy whenever you need it. It is invaluable for charging up your energy reserves before you start your evening, before you enter a challenging meeting, before you out for your aerobics class or whenever else you need a boost. Entering your House on the Right Bank, stepping under your Shower and standing on the Energizing Beam are also the first things you do when you have finished that challenging meeting, dug the garden or done anything else that leaves you wishing you had more energy.

The Energizing Beam has another important role to play in maintaining your physical health: It will rid you of the manifestations of stress, such as a headache, indigestion, backache, neck ache, the first snuffles of a cold, and any other niggling complaints you might suffer from.

Before you use the Energizing Beam in this way, the first thing you must do is admit to yourself that you have a physical complaint. Let's say you've just noticed that you're developing a scratchy throat and a runny nose. Instead of reaching into the medicine cupboard or stocking up on tissues, find a quiet place. If necessary go to the loo (which I call 'the alpha closet'), close the door, and do the exercise in there. You will not be disturbed and no one will know what you're doing in there.

Many people who have come on the MindStore courses, or read my first book, have told me that using the Shower and the Energizing Beam has made a tremendous difference to their health. These two techniques have helped them to reduce their high blood pressure, make migraines a thing of the past, and cure digestive ailments and other complaints. The positive results on their bodies have enabled their doctors to reduce or even stop the drugs they were taking for stress-related illnesses. I am not recommending that you throw away all your pills without consulting your doctor first, but once you start practising these MindStore techniques, the benefits will be more than evident and your doctor will be delighted with your progress. And so will you!

For most of us, all we need do to keep ourselves healthy is to spend five minutes doing the Standard Entry Exercise three times a day. However, if you are suffering from a serious condition or have just come out of hospital, you will get more benefit if you spend 15 minutes on the exercise three times a day. The results will be phenomenal.

As with the other two exercises you have already done, you may find it most effective to record the following on tape and listen to it while you do the exercise, ask a friend to read the exercise to you, or read it through, memorize as much of it as possible and then follow it in your mind.

EXERCISE THREE:

THE ENTRANCE VESTIBULE AND CONDITIONING GYM

Find a comfortable position in your chair, close your eyes and begin breathing slowly and regularly. You will now begin to focus your mind and body on relaxing into a healthy state of being. Once again, as each part of the body is mentioned, concentrate on it and focus your thinking on producing relaxation.

Take a deep breath and relax ... take another deep breath and relax ... take a deep breath and again relax ... My scalp is relaxed, I feel my scalp relaxed ... My forehead is relaxed, I feel my forehead relaxed ... My eyelids are relaxed, I feel my eyelids relaxed ... My face is relaxed, I feel my face relaxed ... My tongue is relaxed, I feel my tongue relaxed ... My jaw is relaxed, I feel my jaw relaxed ... My throat is relaxed, I feel my throat relaxed ...

My shoulders are relaxed, I feel my shoulders relaxed ... My arms and hands are relaxed, I feel my arms and hands relaxed ... My upper back is relaxed, I feel my upper back relaxed ... My chest is relaxed, I feel my chest relaxed ... My lower back is relaxed, I feel my lower back relaxed ...

My abdomen is relaxed, I feel my abdomen relaxed ... My hips are relaxed, I feel my hips relaxed ... My thighs are relaxed, I feel my thighs relaxed ... My knees are relaxed, I feel my knees relaxed ... My calves are relaxed, I feel my calves relaxed ... My ankles are relaxed, I feel my ankles relaxed ... My toes are relaxed, I feel my toes relaxed ... My soles are relaxed, I feel my soles relaxed ... My heels are relaxed, I feel my heels relaxed ...

Take a deep breath and relax ... I will now imagine that I am in a very special place of relaxation ... I am there ... I can see the scene all around me ... I can smell the scent in the air and I can hear all the wonderful sounds ... I will give myself a short period to enjoy this fully [pause for approx. 20 to 30 seconds] ...

Once again I take a deep breath and relax ... I will now adjust and imagine that I am standing on a river bank ... The river is behind me and I am facing a wonderful landscape ...

I can feel my feet on the lush green grass ... overhead the

sky is blue and the air is fresh with the scent of the meadow ...
I can hear the sounds of this wonderful land before me ...

I now look towards my house and remind myself of its
construction, the features of the walls, the red roof and the
entrance area ... I move forward now to stand at the entrance
... in a moment I will open the door to create my Entrance
Vestibule and to place there a symbol of my potential ...

I now open the door ... first of all I create the shape of this
room and the height of the ceiling ... now the decorative fea-
tures, colours and lighting ... In a moment I will place here a
symbol of my potential ... I will trust my creativity and what
comes to mind ... I will pass through the Entrance Vestibule in
all future exercises as part of the Standard Entry Exercise ... I
am programming at foundation level ... In a moment I will cre-
ate my Conditioning Gym ... a room I will use for the fine-tun-
ing of my energy and for relief from the effects of stress ...

The Conditioning Gym is attached to the Entrance
Vestibule ... I now create the shape of the gym and the height
of the ceiling ... now the decorative features, colours and light-
ing ... I will now install a showering area for cleansing nega-
tive energy and its underlying destructive thought patterns ...
I decide on its shape and dimensions ... I select its colours ...
I now place the shower head and a control unit for regulating
its flow ... I will use this showering area in all future exercises
and practice sessions ...

In a moment I will stand within my Shower and cleanse
away any negativity and underlying thought patterns ...

I now enter my showering area and turn on the flow so
that its imaginary cleansing action can commence ... I feel the
warm spring waters running over my hair and down every
inch of my body, draining away mental fatigue and restoring
vibrant life ...

I now imagine the bright sunlight reaching deep within ... filtering out and washing away all my limiting and destructive attitudes, particularly my negative thoughts ...

Readjusting and turning off the Shower I now step out, instantly dry, and fresh with positive expectations ...

I will now create my Energizing Beam, which rises up from a platform on the floor ... I will use this vibrating beam to take away the physical manifestations of stress and for instant access to increased personal energy ...

I have now created my Conditioning Gym ... it will become an integral part of my MindStore techniques as I make them an important part of my life ...

I will now leave the house and return to the river's edge ... I feel the lush green grass beneath my feet ... Soon I will count from 1 to 7, and gradually adjust to come out of this healthy state of deep relaxation ...

1 ... 2 ... 3 ... 4 ... now, beyond the midpoint, when I open my eyes I will be wide awake and revitalized both physically and mentally ... 5, I begin to adjust my body ... 6, I prepare to open my eyes ... and 7, I open my eyes and am wide awake now, both physically and mentally alert.

I recommend that you practise using your Energizing Beam whenever you wish, particularly before a time when you want to have extra energy to carry out a task such as driving home safely on a long journey. I have not included using it in the exercises here (nor do we practise it on the MindStore courses), because it is for you to use as and when you need it.

The Central Hallway

In the following exercise you are going to create the Central Hallway in your House on the Right Bank. You will enter it immediately you leave the Conditioning Gym in all future exercises and practice sessions. As you might expect, this hallway leads to all the other rooms in your house. However, please do not allow your creative imagination to be limited by the word 'hallway'. It does not have to be small like the hallways you find in most houses. It can be vast. For instance, my Central Hallway is certainly *not* a narrow corridor; it's an open-plan piazza with all kinds of people milling about in it. There are spiral staircases and futuristic lifts and escalators that move me towards new possibilities. As you become more experienced with the MindStore techniques you can make your Central Hallway bigger if you want, you can push the walls out – just do whatever your right brain wants.

There is something very positive about this hallway – it is going to record some of the best moments in your life, to remind you of what a unique and very special person you are. You will take those moments that have been special in your life and put a record of them on the walls in the Central Hallway. As you develop the techniques in this book you will remember more and more moments that are special, and will start to build up a gallery of images that reflects the real you. It will be an amazing, phenomenal place, and every time you walk through it you will be filled with joy and pride in your achievements. And, of course, as you start to achieve even more with the help of your MindStore techniques, you will have more magical moments to record. Now you know why your Central Hallway needs to be big and spacious – you are going to want a lot of wall space!

Whenever you review these images in alpha/theta state, you will be restating to yourself that you have experienced happiness, success and achievement in the past and that you will do so again in the future. It is a simple idea but it will have an enormously empowering effect on your self-esteem and therefore on the way you deal with others. As well as these special images, you can also arrange various objects and pieces of furniture in your hallway if you wish.

When you read the exercise through before doing it, you will see that we are now starting to spend less time on the relaxation part of the Standard Entry Exercise. That is because by now your brain is getting the message. It knows that when you sit comfortably in your chair with both feet on the floor and your hands lying loosely in your lap, and you close your eyes and take three deep breaths, your body is going to relax. That is the reason for having such a definite structure to the exercises – it helps to programme your brain. You will also see that slightly less time than before is spent in the landscape of abundance, because by now you are getting accustomed to what it looks like. You no longer need to be given time to create the landscape because it is now in your head. Each time you do these exercises you will take less and less time over them. That does not mean I want you to get into a race with yourself, timing yourself to see how quickly you can do the exercises, but it does mean you will be able to switch into alpha/theta mode quickly whenever you need to.

Now we will start the Exercise Four. As before, you may prefer to dictate the exercise to a tape recorder, or ask a friend to read it out loud.

EXERCISE FOUR: THE CENTRAL HALLWAY

Find a comfortable position in your chair, close your eyes and begin breathing in a regular and slow manner. You will now begin to focus your mind and body on relaxing into a healthy state of being. Once again, as each part of your body is mentioned, concentrate on it and focus your thinking on producing relaxation.

Take a deep breath and relax ... take another deep breath and relax ... take a deep breath and again relax ... My scalp is relaxed, I feel my scalp relaxed ... My forehead is relaxed, I feel my forehead relaxed ... My eyelids are relaxed, I feel my eyelids relaxed ... My face is relaxed, I feel my face relaxed ... My tongue is relaxed, I feel my tongue relaxed ... My jaw is relaxed, I feel my jaw relaxed ... My throat is relaxed, I feel my throat relaxed ...

My shoulders are relaxed, I feel my shoulders relaxed ... My arms and hands are relaxed, I feel my arms and hands relaxed ... My upper back is relaxed, I feel my upper back relaxed ... My chest is relaxed, I feel my chest relaxed ... My lower back is relaxed, I feel my lower back relaxed ...

My abdomen is relaxed, I feel my abdomen relaxed ... My hips are relaxed, I feel my hips relaxed ... My thighs are relaxed, I feel my thighs relaxed ... My knees are relaxed, I feel my knees relaxed ... My calves are relaxed, I feel my calves relaxed ... My ankles are relaxed, I feel my ankles relaxed ... My toes are relaxed, I feel my toes relaxed ... My soles are relaxed, I feel my soles relaxed ... My heels are relaxed, I feel my heels relaxed ...

Take a deep breath and relax ... I will now imagine that I am in a very special place of relaxation ... I am there ... I can see the scene all around me ... I can smell the scent in the air and I can hear all the wonderful sounds ... I will give myself a short period to enjoy this fully [pause for approx. 20 to 30 seconds] ...

Once again I take a deep breath and relax ... I will now adjust and imagine that I am standing on a river bank ... The river is behind me and I am facing a wonderful landscape ...

I can feel my feet on the lush green grass ... overhead the sky is blue and the air is fresh with the scent of the meadow ... I can hear the sounds of this wonderful land before me ...

I now look towards my house and remind myself of its construction, the features of the walls, the red roof and the entrance area ... I move forward now and into my Entrance Vestibule, past my Symbol of Potential and on into my Conditioning Gym ...

In a moment I will stand within my Shower and cleanse away any negativity and underlying thought patterns ...

I now enter my showering area and turn on the flow so that its imaginary cleansing action can commence ... I feel the warm spring waters running down my hair and over every inch of my body, draining away mental fatigue and restoring vibrant life ...

I now imagine the bright sunlight reaching deep within ... filtering out and washing away all my limiting and destructive attitudes, particularly my negative thoughts ...

Readjusting and turning off the Shower I now step out, instantly dry, and fresh with positive expectations ...

In a moment I will create my Central Hallway ... This leads to all the other rooms of my inner home and is accessed directly from the Conditioning Gym ... I now create its shape and the height of the ceiling ... Now the decorative features, colours and lighting ...

On the wall I will now place images depicting times from my past when I have been at my very best [pause for approx. 1 minute] ...

I have now created my Central Hallway ... it leads to all the other rooms in my inner home ...

I will now leave the house and return to the river's edge ... I feel the lush green grass beneath my feet ... Soon I will count from 1 to 7, and gradually adjust to come out of this healthy state of deep relaxation ...

1 ... 2 ... 3 ... 4 ... now, beyond the midpoint, when I open my eyes I will be wide awake and revitalized both physically and mentally ... 5, I begin to adjust my body ... 6, I prepare to open my eyes ... and 7, I open my eyes and am wide awake now, both physically and mentally alert.

Before I end this chapter I would like to tell you of the remarkable experience of Helen Nelson, a Scots MindStore member, when she created her House on the Right Bank. I will let her tell the story:

> I accessed the right bank of the river by crossing an arched stone bridge. My river was curiously still.
>
> There had always been talk of an Irish connection in my family's history, and I had always wondered if it had been a myth built up over the years ... The day before I, my son and husband went on holiday to Ireland in 1994, I confirmed through census records held in Edinburgh Central Library that my great-grandfather did indeed come from Ireland.
>
> I visited his village and was astonished to find a bridge the same as the one in my 'vision', crossing a still body of water (a canal), and on the other bank facing the canal was my House on the Right Bank, just as I had visualized it – and it didn't have a red roof! (I have to confess that I have never been able to see a red roof when I visit my right bank anyway!) The surrounding countryside was soft and peaceful, with no traffic or aircraft noise. There was only the sound of birds singing, the

smell of new-mown hay and a stillness and warmth in the air that was magical.

This experience has brought me very close to my great-grandfather and to the land and people of Ireland, to the extent that if I was compelled to uproot myself from Scotland it would be to settle in Ireland, where I feel very much at one and at home.

3

Improving Your Communications

The most challenging thing we have to deal with in life is communication. Unless we lock ourselves away in an ivory tower or go to live on a desert island, we have to communicate with other people. It's a very important part of being alive. We have to communicate not only on a social level with our friends and family, but also with colleagues, bosses, people in shops, bus conductors, people whose job it is to help us (such as doctors) ... the list is endless. Usually communication is something we take for granted, unless there are medical reasons which make it particularly difficult.

Yet we have all had days when communicating with others has been a challenge, those days when what you want to say comes out backwards, you mean one thing but seem to be saying another, or you begin to wonder if you've become invisible because people simply do not listen to you. It can be frustrating enough when you are struggling to communicate with your partner or child over what time to have supper or when to go shopping; it can have very serious effects when it's your bank manager or boss with whom you are unable to communicate.

It is for times like these that I have developed a number of exciting techniques that will enable you to improve your communications in ways that will have powerful and far-reaching effects on your life, helping you to work harmoniously with other people, express yourself clearly and articulately, and ensure that negotiations and meetings have the best results for everyone concerned.

The Three Ways of Thinking

Scientists have discovered that we have three different ways of thinking – visual, audio and kinaesthetic. Visual people think in pictures and images – they will be able to see their House on the Right Bank quite clearly. Audio people think in sounds – they may not be able to see their House on the Right Bank perfectly but, like me, they will know which floorboards creak, what the Shower sounds like, and so on. Kinaesthetic people think with physical sensations and emotions – they may not be able to see the House on the Right Bank either, but they know what the doorknobs feel like, how warm the water in the Shower is, what the Energizing Beam feels like. Although everyone is able to think in all three ways, most of us find that one way of thinking predominates.

Energy Fields

Whenever I stand on a stage at a MindStore course, I can really feel the energy coming from the audience. I feel I could reach out and touch it. It is the same flow of energy that you get between any live performer and his or her audience, and it is very powerful indeed. In fact, when we do the foundation exercises on these courses, the MindStore members tell me that they have very powerful experiences while visiting their House on the Right Bank. You might think that people would find it a challenge to relax properly in a room of maybe 600 or more people, yet they tell me they find it easy because they can tune in to the collective energy in the room.

It is a well-known fact that the brain is fired by electrical impulses. Every time we think, neurones in the brain send messages to other neurones, either using neuro-transmitters, which are chemicals, or electrical currents. It is also becoming increasingly accepted that our bodies emit a field of electro-magnetic energy, which some people call an aura. Kirlian photography is a special process designed to capture this aura on film, and the colour photographs I have seen of people's auras are quite stunning and also very beautiful in their own right. Some people are able to see auras with their own eyes, and that is a technique I am busy working on – because I want to be able to see them too!

Recently there was a lot of excitement in the media about the research being conducted at Houston University in Texas. Researchers had started to wonder whether thoughts are things. They considered all the so-called coincidences that happen in our lives, such as hearing the phone ring and knowing who is on the other end before you pick it up (sometimes even knowing that the phone's about to ring before it does); or strolling along the road thinking about someone you haven't seen for a while, then turning the corner and walking slap bang into him. And how often have you said, 'Wow, I was just thinking about you!'? We have all experienced coincidences like this at some time or other, and I believe that people who say they haven't simply haven't been paying attention! Well, the researchers in Texas wondered if they could monitor brain wave activity to find evidence of all these things happening. They wired up lots of people to electro-encephalograms, told them to think about the same things at the same time, and studied the printouts. At first nothing matched, and the brain waves were completely random, until someone came up with a fantastic solution – why not study the brain waves of people who love each other and who claim to have experienced these telepathic links? So they started studying mothers and sons, fathers and daughters, husbands and wives, boyfriends and girlfriends – and the results were phenomenal. When they asked two people who loved each other to think about one another, the pattern of their brain waves was identical. The researchers moved them into different rooms and tried again – the results were the same. Even when they separated a couple by more than 2,000 miles and told them to think about each other, the pattern of their brain waves matched perfectly.

I firmly believe that we all produce brain waves that are identical to those of the people we love. They may not have been measured by those Texan researchers, but that does not mean they do not exist. We already know of other ways that thoughts are things. Psychokinesis is the ability to influence matter using the mind, and if you have ever seen people doing this you will know how powerful it is. A famous Russian medium called Nelya Mikhailova apparently made a reporter's sandwich crawl across a desk and topple on to the floor, purely through the power of thought. Can you imagine how you would feel if someone did that with your lunch? In the West, the most famous exponent of psychokinesis is Uri Geller, who made his name in the early 1970s by bending spoons and re-starting the nation's broken watches and clocks, although he is capable of even more amazing feats than that. Scientists have tested Uri's electro-magnetic field and found that it increases considerably when he concentrates on bending or moving metal objects. They have also studied the metal objects themselves, and some tests have revealed that the metal has been put under an extraordinary stress. For Uri, thoughts are most definitely things, and he has an astonishing control over his brain. Yet he says that everyone has the ability to do what he does, if only they would tap into it.

I am quite convinced that if our thoughts about loved ones can be mirrored by their thoughts about us, and that if we can influence objects with our thoughts, then all our thoughts have a powerful effect on us as well. And that goes for negative thoughts as well as positive ones. In his fantas-tic, ground-breaking book, *The Celestine Prophesy*, James Redfield describes the way people's energy fields interact when they communicate with one another. He describes how their energy fields flow together when they like each other, and how a bully's energy will completely envelop other peo-ple's energy fields. He also describes how to teach yourself to be able to see these energy fields, or auras, yourself. Of course, just because you can't see someone's aura does not mean it is not there, just as the fact that you cannot see radio waves whizzing through the air does not mean your radio is unable to receive them.

Not long ago I saw a TV programme about the Rolling Stones' latest world tour, and they were being asked about their music and how they write their songs. I was fascinat-ed and really excited when I heard Keith Richards say that he believes new songs are flying through the air all the time, and all he has to do is catch them. Next time you listen to a Stones song, you might like to imagine that it first started life as a few notes shooting around Keith Richards' head.

The Boomerang Effect

If our thought waves are things, it means that communicating can be much simpler than it currently is for many people. In fact, it's incredibly simple – think positive, constructive thoughts about people and they will respond with positive, constructive results. In other words, as you give, so shall you receive. The Bible talks about this idea, as do all the other major religions of the world. The Buddhist concept of karma is exactly the same idea, couched in different language. And once you have grasped the notion that thoughts are things, you will never again want to send out negative, ugly thoughts because you will know how much damage they will do to you. Negative thinking about someone will come straight back at you, just like a boomerang.

Programming Your Future Histories

In this chapter I am going to introduce you to a fantastic technique that will improve your communications with other people for ever. It will give you the ability and the knowledge to create constructive relationships that will work for you for as long as they last. By the way, I am not talking about discovering how to weld someone to your side for ever, because this technique is not about having power over someone else. It is about learning to communicate with someone at thought level so that the result is best for all concerned.

Incidentally, I believe that we all have to recognize that not every relationship is going to last for ever. Some people believe that if a relationship ends, it has been a failure. I do not agree at all. I believe that we meet people because we need them for some reason, whether we are aware of it at the time or not, and when that relationship moves on it is because we no longer need each other. What is important is to enjoy the time you have together.

The technique that I am about to describe will enable you to improve your communications by leaps and bounds, because you will mentally rehearse what you are going to say, how meetings will go, how interviews will turn out – before they take place. It is an incredibly powerful tool and one that I use every day of my life. I not only use it for communications but for setting goals (something I describe in great detail in my previous book, *MindStore*). In this book we are going to use this technique for improving communications, but the process is exactly the same and, once you start using it, it will change your life for ever.

When I was a young kid, I remember my father dragging me out of bed one night to go downstairs and watch TV. I had been fast asleep and I didn't want to leave my warm bed, but in the end he persuaded me, and sat me down in front of the TV. There was Michael Parkinson talking to Muhammad Ali. Ali was repeating his marvellous catch-phrase, 'I am the greatest.' My father asked me what Ali was *not* saying, but I was still wiping the sleep out of my eyes, so he had to tell me – what Ali was *not* saying was 'One day I'll be the greatest.' He was saying that he already was the greatest.

Ali created what he called 'future histories' for himself. The moment he would sign a contract for a fight, he would go home, relax completely, and then mentally rehearse every single moment that would take him up to the success-ful conclusion of that fight. He would use all his senses for this: he would smell the liniment and sweat, would hear the crowd yelling his name, would feel his gum shield in his mouth and the bandages wrapped around his hands. His body would feel every punch from his opponent, and his fists would feel every punch he delivered in return. He would mentally rehearse the whole fight until the final moment, when the referee would grab his arm and declare him the winner. He called it 'future history' because he was looking into the future but it was also as if he had already lived through it, in his imagination and with absolute clarity. And he didn't only do it once – Ali would live through his future history every night and every morning leading up to a fight.

Did you notice that I said Ali relaxed himself completely before mentally rehearsing his next fight? He didn't need to do the MindStore course to know that his future histories would have the most impact on his brain when it was in alpha/theta mode.

In Exercise Five I will show you how to create a special room in your House on the Right Bank, a room that I call the Editing Suite. In this room you will be able to review your current situation, assess and analyse it, view alternatives, and then focus on the solution in a way that will create positive change in your life.

Assessing the Challenge

Whenever you are faced with a challenge, whether it comes in the form of a big gas bill, an uncooperative child or a difficult neighbour, there are four logical steps involved in solving it:

1   You have to **admit** and **accept** that the challenge exists. Once you do, you are more than halfway towards finding a solution.
2   **Analyse** the situation. If you do this when your brain is in its wide awake, beta state, you will be viewing

the situation in a very logical way. But if you do it in alpha/theta, you may see things in a whole new light.

3   Look at the **alternatives**. Consider the scenario and see you how feel about it, and then carry on until you have considered all the options. Once you have done this, logic tells us that one of them must be the solution.

4   **Focus** all your energy on the solution. You are no longer looking back into your past at the challenge, you are now looking forward into the future and the solution. And that is an incredibly powerful position to be in.

The Editing Suite

I will now teach you how to create the new room in your House on the Right Bank which you will visit whenever you want to solve a challenge in your life, or programme your future history. I call it the Editing Suite because it is here that you will edit your past and also edit your current reality and future histories.

When you walk into the room you will create an enormous wall, on which will be three gigantic cinema screens. These aren't the usual size, they are absolutely colossal. The cinema screen on the right will always show your past, the central screen will always show your present, and the screen on the left will always show your future.

Opposite the central screen you will place a beautifully comfortable chair – you can make it a director's chair if you like, because from this moment on you are the director of your life. Next to the chair is a video machine with an aerial for broadcasting and receiving. This aerial is very important because it will receive all kinds of essential information; your intuition will be able to make use of this information and will be able to draw on it when making decisions. Once you start using the Editing Suite, you will realize this for your-self. The Suite also contains a remote-control handset for operating the video machine and the three cinema screens.

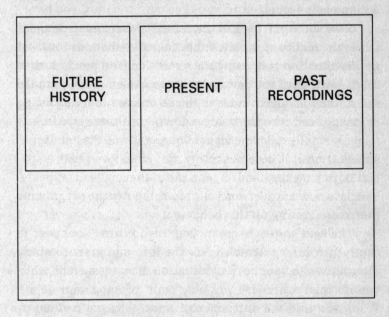

You will use the Editing Suite after visiting your Conditioning Gym in the usual way. Then you will sit in your chair, put a video in the machine and switch on the central screen.

You will bring up on the screen a relationship that is not happy, that needs improvement. You admit and accept it. If you find that you are experiencing negative feelings towards the person concerned, such as disappointment, sadness or anger, then you pick up the remote-control handset and turn down the volume of what you are hearing, or shrink the picture so it becomes smaller. You will find that when you do this you no longer feel so threatened and are more in control.

You then switch on the past screen, which is the one on the right, and analyse the challenge you face. When did it happen, why did it happen, how did it happen? As I have already explained, because you are using both hemispheres of your brain for this, you may come up with an insight that will present a solution.

Now you come back to the centre screen and once again admit the reality of the situation. Take the emotions involved in this situation and, using the remote-control handset, turn them down until you can no longer feel them. Then you take the sounds involved, such as raised voices, angry shouting or crying, and turn the volume down until there is absolute silence. Finally, take the visual image and use the handset to shrink it until it becomes a tiny dot, when you press a special button on the handset, and *ping!* the image disappears. You have now erased from your bio-computer the programme that keeps setting up this behaviour.

The next step is to create your own future. Look over to the future screen, which is on the left, and start to study alternatives to your current situation. Be very specific when you do this, otherwise you may omit an important detail. When you find the outcome you want, that you feel happy with, you do what Muhammad Ali did. Using the handset, you make the scene bigger and bigger, and turn up the colour too if you want, until it is absolutely huge. Turn up the volume, too, so you can really hear what's going on. Adjust the tone if you wish, so it sounds deeper or softer. And then really turn up the emotions involved, really *feel* them. Now freeze-frame it and surround it with brilliant white light. Look at your future history and know, with desire, belief and expectation, that it is yours. Don't worry about how you are going to achieve this; just know that you will. Now press another button on the handset and let the image be transmitted out into the world, so that people, places and opportunities can pick it up and come to your aid. The desire for this goal will get you going, the belief in it will keep you going, and the expectation will act like a magnet and attract what you need to achieve your goal.

At this point I always add a final message: 'May the best for all involved occur.' I say that because what I think is best for me may not be best for the other people concerned. And I don't always achieve the goals I set, yet when I ask myself why a programme did not work, I realize that it was because it was not right for me. I never get upset or feel fazed by it. On the contrary, I learn from it.

Once you have programmed a future history and freeze-framed it on your future screen, never, ever go back through the process. To reinforce the technique, all you need do is review your future screen.

EXERCISE FIVE: THE EDITING SUITE
Find a comfortable position in your chair, close your eyes and begin breathing slowly and regularly. You will now begin to focus your mind and body on relaxing into a healthy state of being. Once again, as each part of your body is mentioned, concentrate on it and focus your thinking on producing relaxation.

Take a deep breath and relax ... take another deep breath and relax ... take a deep breath and again relax ... My scalp is relaxed, I feel my scalp relaxed ... My forehead is relaxed, I feel my forehead relaxed ... My eyelids are relaxed, I feel my eyelids relaxed ... My face is relaxed, I feel my face relaxed ... My tongue is relaxed, I feel my tongue relaxed ... My jaw is relaxed, I feel my jaw relaxed ... My throat is relaxed, I feel my throat relaxed ...

My shoulders are relaxed, I feel my shoulders relaxed ... My arms and hands are relaxed, I feel my arms and hands relaxed ... My upper back is relaxed, I feel my upper back relaxed ... My chest is relaxed, I feel my chest relaxed ... My lower back is relaxed, I feel my lower back relaxed ...

My abdomen is relaxed, I feel my abdomen relaxed ... My hips are relaxed, I feel my hips relaxed ... My thighs are relaxed, I feel my thighs relaxed ... My knees are relaxed, I feel my knees relaxed ... My calves are relaxed, I feel my calves relaxed ... My ankles are relaxed, I feel my ankles relaxed ... My toes are relaxed, I feel my toes relaxed ... My soles are relaxed, I feel my soles relaxed ... My heels are relaxed, I feel my heels relaxed ...

Take a deep breath and relax ... I will now imagine that I am in a very special place of relaxation ... I am there ... I will give myself a short period to enjoy this fully [pause for approx. 20 to 30 seconds] ...

Once again I take a deep breath and relax ... I will now adjust and imagine that I am standing on a river bank ... The river is behind me and I am facing a wonderful landscape ...

I can feel my feet on the lush green grass ... overhead the sky is blue and the air is fresh with the scent of the meadow ... I can hear the sounds of this wonderful land before me ...

I now move forward and through the doorway of my house with the red roof ... into my Entrance Vestibule, past my Symbol of Potential and on into my Conditioning Gym ...

In a moment I will stand within my Shower and cleanse away any negativity and underlying thought patterns ...

I now enter my showering area and turn on the flow, so that its imaginary cleansing action can commence ... I feel the warm spring waters running down my hair and over every inch of my body, draining away mental fatigue and restoring vibrant life ...

I now imagine the bright sunlight reaching deep within ... filtering out and washing away all my limiting and destruc-

tive attitudes, particularly my negative thoughts ...

Readjusting and turning off the Shower I now step out, instantly dry, and fresh with positive expectations ...

In a moment I will create my Editing Suite, which is entered by a doorway off my Central Hallway ... It will be used for problem-solving and goal-setting ...

I now leave my Conditioning Gym and enter my Central Hallway, the walls covered with images depicting times from my past when I have been at my very best ... I now create the room that will house my Editing Suite ... I decide on its shape, the height of the ceiling ... now the decorative features, colours and lighting ... On one of the walls, high up near the ceiling, I will place a time-frame for programming dates ... Suspended on the wall just below the time-frame I now erect three gigantic cinema screens: one in the middle for the now, one to the left for my future histories, and one to the right for my past recordings ...

Facing the central screen I will now install a director's chair ... Now a projector and a remote-control handset for operating the screens ... I will project images onto the screens for the purpose of setting goals and problem-solving ...

In future I will admit and accept that I have a challenge by projecting my current situation on the central screen ... I can go into the past screen on the right to analyse ... By using my remote-control handset I can return to the central screen and turn down the image, feelings and sounds until they almost disappear ... I can then imagine pressing a Delete button to remove the programme completely from the screen ...

Now on the left-hand (future) screen I will explore alternatives before selecting the one I truly want for my life at this time ... I will make it bigger and bigger, bringing it closer to me before freeze-framing it in brilliant white light ... I will then have a future history ...

Regularly reviewing my future histories on the left-hand screen will build my desire, belief, and certainty that I will achieve my goal or desired outcome ...

I have now created my Editing Suite ... I will use it for attracting into my life the people, places and opportunities I need to achieve my goals ...

I will now leave the house and return to the river's edge ... I feel the lush green grass beneath my feet. Soon I will count from 1 to 7, and gradually adjust to come out of this healthy state of deep relaxation ...

1 ... 2 ... 3 ... 4 ... now, beyond the midpoint, when I open my eyes I will be wide awake and revitalized both physically and mentally ... 5, I begin to adjust my body ... 6, I prepare to open my eyes ... and 7, I open my eyes and am wide awake now, both physically and mentally alert.

Tip-of-the-Tongue Trigger

Until now, whenever we have visited the House on the Right Bank we have done so using the Standard Entry Exercise, but there is a quicker way into the house, called the Direct Access Route, which I have developed for those times when you need instant access into the alpha/theta state. I call it the 'tip-of-the-tongue trigger', and I will talk about it in depth in Chapter 7. Here I want to describe simply how to do it (you may want to look at pages 138–43 as well now, before reading on).

Whenever you need to enter your House on the Right Bank quickly, all you do is place the tip of your tongue on the roof of your mouth directly behind your two front teeth. This helps you to gain instant access to your house and whichever room you need; it acts as an anchor for all the communication techniques that follow.

The powerful and dynamic effect this simple technique has on your communications will delight and astound you. In all future exercises and practice sessions you will find that it automatically brings with it all the feelings of relaxation you associate with the MindStore techniques. You will be able to use this triggering device in meetings, when listening to people, when writing important letters and in many other ways (*see* Chapter 7).

The following simple exercise will enable you to programme the use of the tip-of-the-tongue trigger. Ideally, you should always visit your Conditioning Gym and have a Shower to rid yourself of negative thoughts and energies before proceeding to the other rooms in your House on the Right Bank. However, if you are in a hurry or need instant access, all you need do is take three deep breaths and then place the tip of your tongue in position. When you have finished using the tip-of-the-tongue trigger, there is no need to leave your landscape by counting up to seven – simply remove your tongue from its position and carry on with what you were doing.

EXERCISE SIX:
THE TIP-OF-THE-TONGUE TRIGGER/DIRECT ACCESS ROUTE
Place the tip of your tongue directly behind your front two teeth on the roof of your mouth. Doing this throughout the future sessions will build the strength of this trigger so that you associate the tongue in this position with your relaxation and the house with the red roof. Once you have established this (after a few sessions – trust it) you simply do the following to access the house directly:

Take a deep breath and relax ... take another deep breath and relax ... take a deep breath and again relax ...

Gently touch the roof of your mouth, directly behind your two front teeth, with the tip of your tongue. Whenever you use the tip-of-the-tongue trigger like this, you will immediately enter your foundation level and access your faculties of concentration, imagination and intuition. The tip-of-the-tongue trigger is a powerful programming tool which you can use for whatever purpose you desire.

Take a deep breath and relax ... I will now imagine that I am standing on a river bank ... The river is behind me and I am facing a wonderful landscape ...

I can feel my feet on the lush green grass ... overhead the sky is blue and the air is fresh with the scent of the meadow ... I can hear the sounds of this wonderful land before me ...

I now look towards my house and remind myself of its construction, the features of the walls, the red roof and the entrance area ... I move forward now and into my Entrance Vestibule, past my Symbol of Potential and on into my Conditioning Gym ...

In a moment I will stand within my Shower and cleanse away any negativity and underlying thought patterns ...

I now enter my showering area and turn on the flow, so that its imaginary cleansing action can commence ... I feel the warm spring waters running down my hair and over every inch of my body, draining away mental fatigue and restoring vibrant life ...

I now imagine the bright sunlight reaching deep within ... filtering out and washing away all my limiting and destructive attitudes, particularly my negative thoughts ...

Readjusting and turning off the Shower I now step out, instantly dry, and fresh with positive expectations ...

I will now proceed to the other rooms in my House on the Right Bank ...

Hello, Is Anyone Listening?

Have you ever had a long conversation with someone and then realized that he or she hasn't been listening to a word you've said? It's happened to all of us. If you're honest, you will admit that there are times when you don't listen, either. Do you ever watch the news at night and realize, when the weather forecast appears, that you haven't heard a word that's been said for the past half-hour? And has the same thing happened to you in meetings, in important discussions, in interviews? You've started thinking about the strange pattern on a colleague's tie, or wondering if you can get home before the rush-hour starts, or hoping that you won't be asked about that report you still haven't found time to write.

Scientists have discovered that when you have a conversation with someone, the actual words account for only 7 per cent of what is conveyed between you. The tone of what you are saying carries 35 per cent of the message, and the remaining 58 per cent consists of non-verbal communication, such as the speaker's body language and facial expressions.

I've thought about this a lot and have decided that I can't afford to trust that I am understanding someone's tone correctly, hearing his or her words and interpreting his or her body language correctly. Communication is too important to leave to chance, so I decided to develop techniques that worked while I was accessing more of the faculties of my whole brain in order to give me an edge.

The following techniques will help you to make the most of your communications so you get the very best out of every phone call, every meeting, every party, every chance encounter.

Meeting the Needs of Others

As I explained earlier in this chapter, relationships are all about people's needs. Some relationships are more satisfactory than others because they meet our needs, others fall short of satisfying our needs.

You can use the following technique to think very creatively about how to focus on your needs in your relationships, and also the needs of the other person or people concerned. You can do it either by following the Standard Entry Exercise or using the Direct Access Route, keeping your tongue above your two front teeth all the time.

In your imagination, enter the Editing Suite and remind yourself of its layout. Sit in the chair and allow yourself to focus on one of the relationships you have in your life. Trust the one that comes to mind. It may be very intimate or it may not be a very significant one; whichever one you think about will be the relationship your subconscious wants to focus on, so let it happen. On your central screen, bring up that relationship. Ask yourself, 'What are the needs of this person?' Now, because you can do anything in your imagination, ask that person what his or her needs are and make up his or her reply. Trust that whatever you think of will be the right answer.

As you begin to identify the other person's needs, go to your past screen and review the recent weeks or months. Ask yourself whether you are meeting this person's needs. If you are, congratulate yourself. If you are not, see what happens and the challenge it creates for that person. Return to the centre screen and admit and accept this.

Now go to the future screen, and see yourself meeting this person's needs. Make a commitment to that relationship now. Freeze-frame the image in brilliant white light.

Now return to the centre screen, see the relationship again and ask yourself what *your* needs are. Be honest! Look to your past screen to see if they are being met. Notice how you feel if they are not. Now return to the centre screen and admit and accept that reality, then programme on your future screen your needs being met by the other person. Feel wonderful about your needs being met and about how the relationship is now growing stronger. Freeze-frame this image in brilliant white light.

Take a deep breath and relax, then count from 1 to 7 in the usual way. When you reach 7, gently open your eyes.

Middle-of-the-Night Programming

This is a very exciting technique! I love talking about it at my courses because it always gets such a good response from the audience. Your logical, left brain will deny that what you are about to read can happen, but your creative, right brain will love it. If you have the nerve to do Middle-of-the-Night Programming, you will find that *it only works*.

Next time you are finding it difficult to deal with someone, or would like to be able to talk things through with him or her properly, it will be most effective if you do it in the middle of the night. Yes, I know the other person won't be around, but you will be able to talk in your imagination. Remember, time does not exist in the alpha/theta state.

Before you go to sleep, tell yourself that you will wake up at the time when the person you want to 'programme' is at his or her most receptive. This might be 1.30 in the morning, 4.15, 5.50 – you won't know when it will be until you wake up. When you wake, get out of bed and go to the loo, then get back into bed and sit up in a comfortable position. (Always sit up to do this because you will stay awake – if you lie down you will probably drift back to sleep again.)

Using the tip-of-the-tongue trigger, enter your Editing Suite and get up on the central screen an image of the person you want to communicate with. Then have a chat. If the person doesn't know you, then do exactly what you would if you met him or her face to face – introduce yourself. Explain why you want to talk, and ask him or her to be open-minded about what you have to say. Remember, we all have free will and you can't programme someone to do something he or she does not want to do – the aim is to ensure that the results are the best for everyone concerned. You are not issuing instructions here, you are simply having a chat with the person at the time when he or she is most receptive.

Then look at your future screen and programme the outcome you desire. You may feel that you are making the whole thing up, but go with it; it is the right feeling to have, so trust what you are making up. Your controlled imagination will be driven by your intuition. Don't forget to add an affirmation, such as 'May the best for all concerned occur.' Go through every stage and freeze-frame the final image, surrounded in brilliant white light.

The next time you see the person, use the tip-of-the-tongue trigger and remember your future history – forget everything from the past, just focus on your positive new relationship. You can then start to enjoy it.

Programming Children

If you are a parent, you are no doubt experiencing all the joys and heartaches of having a child. Norma and I have two sons, Anthony and Christopher – normal, healthy boys doing all the things that normal, healthy boys do. Some of these are more of a challenge to us than others, but we have found that the Editing Suite and Middle-of-the-Night Programming have been invaluable when we need to handle difficult situations. Of course we talk to the boys and discuss what is wrong, but we also programme their future histories so that we can all work towards a positive outcome for them. So, if your child wets his bed, sucks her thumb, is scared of her teacher, frightened of dogs, has a stutter or is experiencing any sort of difficulty, I can assure you that the Editing Suite and Middle-of-the-Night Programming will help you to solve the problem.

I will never forget talking to a successful businessman at a MindStore for Business course in Edinburgh. This guy was big and tough, but he was in tears when he told me about his daughter. When she was 15, something happened between them that made her vow never to speak to him again. And she had kept that vow for three years. Finally, he 'programmed' her in the middle of the night, when she was most receptive. He imagined she was in the room with him. He talked to her and said how sorry he was, explained what had been happening to him at the time, and went back in his imagination to when the incident took place so he could see exactly what he had done. He apologized to her, and then he programmed her forgiveness and the resumption of their relationship. His daughter rang him less than 24 hours later!

How does it happen? Is it thought transference, projecting your thoughts on to others? I don't know. All I do know is that it works, and can achieve phenomenal results, especially when you are dealing with people you love.

Programming for Interviews and Meetings

You can use these MindStore techniques in every area of
your life. I use Middle-of-the-Night Programming before
every business meeting I have, and the results are quite
incredible. In fact, I recently went to Kuwait and the results
were way beyond what I had programmed.

Let me give you an example of how this works, especially if you will be programming people you have never met
before. Let's say that I am having a big meeting tomorrow
with a group of businesspeople. I have only spoken to their
chairman on the telephone, so I haven't got a clue what he
looks like, and I don't know how many members of his team
will be at the meeting. That's OK, because I can let my imagination fill in the gaps. Before I go to sleep the night before,
I tell myself that I will wake up at a time when this group of
people will be most receptive to me. Then, using the techniques that I describe in Chapter 5, I fall into a deep and
refreshing sleep.

At some point in the night I will wake up. Now, I have
already programmed myself to wake up and, because I have
explained the reason for this to myself, I will not simply turn
over and go back to sleep. Instead, I will sit up in bed and,
using the tip-of-the-tongue trigger, enter my Editing Suite.
I will imagine the men and women I am going to meet later.
I will greet them and start talking. I will say something like,
'Hello, my name's Jack Black. I've got a meeting with you all
in the morning.' They smile and reply: 'Oh, yes, we're looking forward to it.' Remember, this is my imagination, so I
can make them say whatever I want! Then I say: 'When I
meet you later on today, I would like you to be open to what
I will tell you.' I am not going to issue them with instructions, I am simply going to request their co-operation. Then

I tell them: 'When I meet you later today, I will be using the tip-of-the-tongue trigger while listening to you, which means my brain will be in alpha/theta and I will be really focused on what you say. When I talk, I will say the right thing for you.' And they say 'Great!'

After that, I move to my future screen and programme the most positive, successful and empowering meeting that these people have ever had. It's such a dynamic meeting that it will knock their socks off. Then I programme them offering me whatever it is I would like – to be asked to run a course for their company, given a contract, or whatever is applicable. I programme us agreeing dates, agreeing fees, agreeing whatever needs to be arranged. I freeze-frame the outcome, then I leave the House on the Right Bank and go back to sleep.

The following day, I arrive at that meeting at least 15 minutes early. I always do this. I don't sit in reception twiddling my thumbs or flicking through the newspaper. I ask if I can use the loo and I spend those 15 minutes in my House on the Right Bank. First I relax myself completely, then I enter my Editing Suite and mentally rehearse the meeting all over again, using my future screen. I take it right up to the point I got to in the Middle-of-the-Night Programming, then I leave my Editing Suite, enter my Conditioning Gym and stand on the Energizing Beam to charge myself up completely. At this point I stand up and take a step forward, while imagining I have just stepped on my Energizing Beam. Then I leave my House on the Right Bank and count to 7 – and only then do I walk out of the loo. I am so charged up that when I walk into that meeting I am full of incredible self-confidence, self-belief and focus, completely ready to do business. What's more, all through that meeting, whenever I am not speaking I use the tip-of-the-tongue trigger to ensure

I am completely tuned in to what everyone is saying. This puts me way ahead of everyone else in that room, unless they also happen to be MindStore members, when of course they will also have programmed me, so we are bound to have an enjoyable and amazingly productive meeting.

If you use these techniques before every meeting and interview, your career will alter dramatically. I have had salespeople on my courses who have reported a five-fold increase in sales after they start using the MindStore techniques. The MindStore techniques have worked for companies such as Glaxo and organizations such as the Metropolitan Police, and they will work for you.

Programming for Enjoyment

These techniques will work not only for important business meetings. They are equally effective for programming parties, receptions, phone calls, first dates, proposals, weddings – you name it, you can programme them all.

Here's a thought: Many people find Christmas a challenge, having to cope with over-excited children, grumpy adults, family tensions and all the other luggage of life that people carry around with them. Instead of worrying in advance about all the things that might go wrong with your Christmas – from forgetting to buy the turkey to having to listen yet again to your uncle running through his repertoire of out-of-tune carols – spend some time programming your Christmas to run smoothly and ensure that everyone has a really good time.

Programme your uncle with the Middle-of-the-Night technique, tactfully asking him to give the carols a rest. Programme the family to volunteer to do the washing up. Programme all the other things you would like to happen.

Programme the best Christmas your family has ever had. Believe me, *it only works*.

Mirroring

Remember when I said that a staggering 58 per cent of our communication consists of non-verbal messages? That means that the way you sit in your chair, the way you hold your head, whether you cross your arms or sit with your hands clasped behind your head – all of it conveys a powerful message to the other person.

In the 1970s there was a tremendous explosion of interest in the study of body language. It was believed that sitting with your arms and legs crossed, for instance, meant that you were feeling vulnerable and wanted to protect yourself in some way. But surely we sometimes sit this way just because it's comfortable? Now, in the 1990s, Neuro-Linguistic Programming (NLP) therapists are saying that people who sit like this, especially if they also have their head tilted to one side, are 'audio thinkers'. So the interpretation of people who sit with their arms and legs crossed has changed: they no longer need to protect themselves; now they are audio thinkers!

We don't yet know which interpretation is correct, but something we *do* know is that people respond favourably to those who look like they do. Obviously if you are dark-haired and you meet someone who is blonde, you are not going to be able to put on a blonde wig suddenly (he or she would probably notice), but what you can do is match your body language to his or hers. If you are chatting while standing up, and the person you are talking to has got his arms folded across his chest, you should fold your arms in exactly the same way. Then, if he shifts his weight from one foot to the other, you should do the same thing. Unless he has read this book or is familiar with NLP, his conscious mind is unlikely to notice what you are doing, but his subconscious mind will cotton on really fast and, what's more, it will really appreciate it. If you can also match the rate at which you speak to his, you'll be onto a winner.

However, what you must never, ever do is mirror someone's affliction. If someone has a limp, a stutter, a facial tic or something equally noticeable, you must not mirror it!

There are times when mirroring is particularly useful. For instance, if someone invites me to have a drink with her after work, or after one of my courses, I will disappear into the old 'alpha closet' or a quiet room somewhere and mentally rehearse the event, using my Editing Suite. If that person says 'Jack, there's someone over here I'd like you to meet,' in the time it takes to walk over to her I can very quickly use the tip-of-the-tongue trigger and mentally programme a good meeting – it need only take seconds. However, if there is absolutely no time in which to rehearse the meeting mentally – such as when I bump into a friend in the street or am unexpectedly introduced to someone – I use mirroring.

Cold Calling

Speaking to people on the telephone can present a big challenge, especially if you have to make a difficult call. You are unable to see the other person, so none of the non-verbal body-language cues can come to your aid. Here are four MindStore techniques that will enable you to maximize your ability to communicate with *anyone* on the telephone:

1   Use the Editing Suite, whenever possible, before
making a phone call. It will only take a minute at the
most to use the tip-of-the-tongue trigger and mentally
rehearse the conversation you are about to have. This
will have a tremendous impact on the success of your
telephone calls – especially those that are likely to
present you with a challenge. You can also use this
technique to rehearse any phone calls you are
expecting to receive.

2   If someone rings you out of the blue, which means you
have not had a chance to programme the conversation,
use the tip-of-the-tongue trigger while listening to the
other person. Use it all the time you are listening; this
will not only improve your ability to listen to what that
person has to say, but will improve your capacity to
respond in an intuitive way, guaranteeing you the best
results.

3   As I explained earlier in this chapter, there are visual
thinkers, audio thinkers and kinaesthetic thinkers.
Visual people tend to speak really fast in their attempt
to keep pace with all the images flashing through their
heads. Kinaesthetic people have to translate all the
sensations and emotions they are experiencing into
words, so it can take some time for them to express
themselves. Audio thinkers speak at an average pace.
You can imagine what happens when a visual thinker
and a kinaesthetic thinker talk to each other over the
phone: nine times out of ten the visual thinker will
finish all the kinaesthetic thinker's sentences for him
or her, something guaranteed to drive both of them
absolutely nuts before long. So, from now on, when you
speak to someone on the telephone the first thing you
need to do is listen to the pace at which the person is

speaking and match it immediately. As usual,
use the tip-of-the-tongue trigger when listening,
then speak at the same pace as the other person.

4 If you experience difficulties with someone on the
telephone, or if you can sense that the other person
is very nervous, het up or angry, close your eyes
and use the tip-of-the-tongue trigger to send them
a soothing psychic message such as 'I love you,'
'I'm on your side' or 'It's OK.' It only works, as
you will find out if you try it.

Of course, you won't use these techniques only when you
are on the telephone. They are just as effective when you are
talking to someone face to face, when you can also use mirroring.

By combining all these techniques you will have a powerful repertoire of tools that will improve your communications in fantastic ways.

4

Improving Your Memory and Ability to Learn

Imagination is more important than knowledge.

ALBERT EINSTEIN

How good do you think your memory is? Are you able to remember names, places and dates with ease, or is it sometimes a challenge even to recall what you had for lunch yesterday? If so, take heart, because you are in the majority – most people wish their memory were better. And it can be – current research is giving us a phenomenal insight into how the mind works and ways to improve memory.

How the Brain Remembers Things

Until the microscope was developed, the brain was regarded as a lump of soft, grey matter that did not do much other than enable us to function. No one placed much importance on the brain. Once scientists were able to examine the brain in detail, however, and as their equipment became more sophisticated, they discovered that it is full of tiny neurones (the current understanding is that each brain contains 300 billion individual cells and neurones). What is more, each neurone looks like a baby octopus, with masses of tentacles radiating off it; the surface of each tentacle is studded with minute fingers. It is currently believed that every one of these 300 billion cells can house up to 1,000 pieces of information, and will continue to function like this throughout our lives.

I am sure you have heard older people saying that their memory isn't as good as it used to be. Some even say it with relish, as if they're pleased to have an excuse not to use their brains anymore. However, unless there is an organic change to the brain caused by disease or injury, it is a complete myth that the older we get, the worse our memory becomes. In fact, if you keep working at your memory, exercising it just as you would any other part of your body that you wish to keep in shape, those tentacles in your brain will keep growing new, tiny fingers that reach out to other tiny fingers and make more connections. In other words, your memory will improve because your brain will physically improve.

To give you some idea of the incredible amount of information the brain can store, imagine an ordinary garden pea sitting next to a human brain. The space taken up in that brain by the little pea would contain all the information you need to telephone every number in the world. It gives a whole new meaning to the term 'pea-brained'!

Recording for Posterity

The latest research suggests that every single thing that happens to us in our lives is recorded by our brain. And I am not just talking about the big things, like your first day at school, the afternoon you fell off your bike and broke your arm, or your wedding day – I am talking about every single incident that has taken place in your life. People who have nearly died and whose lives have flashed before their eyes say that they saw *everything* that ever happened to them.

Of course, not of all of this information is important, so it doesn't matter if, under everyday circumstances, you are unable to recall what colour your toothbrush was when you were 12 years old – but it does matter if you can't remember where you put a spare set of keys, the name of your new boss, or anything about an important piece of research you spent hours reading.

It is not your memory that lets you down when things like this happen, it is your recall system that has failed. The information has been stored away somewhere in your brain – the big challenge is finding a way to retrieve it. So, if remembering things poses a challenge for you, then you need to find a way of improving your powers of recollection.

The first way we all learned to remember things was through repetition. This was how we were taught to speak, and how we later learned our mathematical tables and how to conjugate French, German and Latin verbs at school. It worked fine, but wasn't it boring? Many of us, by the time we are adults, tend to associate learning with endless repetition and with being told off when we got it wrong. No wonder we aren't keen on learning anything new by the time we reach adulthood! The luggage of life that we all carry tells us that learning is a trial, a bore or (if you were thwacked with your Latin teacher's belt, as I was, whenever you got something wrong) literally a pain.

There are already plenty of techniques for improving your memory, including one that involves creating mental associations for the things you want to remember. For instance, if you want to remember the name of your new boss, you should find a way of creating a link between her name and something that is memorable about her. So, if her name is Rosemary Carr, you might imagine that she's sitting in a car absolutely stuffed full with huge sprigs of rosemary, or you might think 'Rosemary is the herb of remembrance, so when I see her I will remember that she is Rosemary.'

These techniques certainly work, but I have found on my courses that, although most people have heard of them, only a tiny fraction actually use them. This is because they are too much like hard work.

I have developed techniques to help you to improve the way you feed information into your brain, so you will be better able to recall it whenever you need it. If you use all the tools and techniques in this chapter you will stand head and shoulders above everyone else, especially if you are currently studying a subject or revising for exams. They will serve you just as well if you need to read and remember books or reports for your job, or want to stay ahead of the game in business. These techniques will give you absolute power over your mind, but you will only be able to use them if you really want them to work.

Desire, Belief, and Certainty

If you are going to use any of the techniques in this book, you must first have the *desire* to do well. You build this desire by focusing on the benefits that will come to you as a result of doing whatever it is you want to do. What would be the benefits of passing that exam with flying colours? What would be the benefits of going to that meeting and remembering everything that is said? What would be the benefits of reading that book and adding to your store of information?

You then need *belief*. You need to believe that these techniques work. You might be thinking 'It's OK for Jack, he's been doing this for years. But how can I trust that it will work?' Well, when I began using all these techniques I was in the same boat. I had no proof that they would work, but I told myself that they would – and they did. In fact, they worked phenomenally well, and still do. It will be the same for you. All you need to do is tell yourself that what you are doing will work, and whenever any self-doubt creeps in you say to yourself, 'Delete that programme, this will work.' It's as simple as that.

Finally, you need *certainty*. Every person I've ever met who has succeeded has said, 'I always knew I would do it' or 'I have always dreamed that this would happen.' They were sure in their expectations, and things worked out as planned.

Desire is the energy that kicks you off in the direction of your goal. Belief is the energy that keeps you going when things get tough – not many people are an instant success and, even if they are, they are usually unprepared for it, and may by destroyed by it. Certainty pulls you slowly but surely towards your goal. It may take some time, but you will get there, I guarantee it.

The Library of Knowledge

If you have ever had to re-read a paragraph, or even a chapter, of a book several times because your mind has been on other things, you will know how frustrating this can be. Most of us give up trying to read the book and put it down, never to pick it up again. This might be OK if you are reading solely for entertainment, because it may not matter greatly if you never read it. But what do you do if it's something that can really help you, either personally or professionally? You can either carry on as before, which I call 'open-ended reading' – stopping whenever you are interrupted and hoping that some of the information stays in your brain – or you can develop a special technique, which I call 'close-ended reading'. The technique involves a very special room, called the Library of Knowledge, in your House on the Right Bank.

Einstein said that 'the things that can be measured don't count, and the things that can't be measured *do* count'. In other words, everything that we have done before, everything from the past, means nothing – it is the future that matters. And the future only happens in your imagination – by the time you experience it, it will actually be the present. Look around you; everywhere you see things that began life in someone's imagination. Before they existed, every object had to be imagined first, from bottled water (and what a great idea that was) to carrots (someone had to think of planting them before they started to grow, and of creating new varieties). Thoughts are things, remember.

Exercise Seven (*see page 93*) describes how to create the Library of Knowledge in your House on the Right Bank. Once you have created it, you can use it for the rest of your life whenever you want to learn by reading. But first let's talk generally about what it will look like and how it will help you.

It is a very special library, with a lecture hall at one end (consisting of a stage with a few chairs ranged in front of it) and a beautiful desk and comfortable chair at the other. All around the walls of the library are bookshelves, and the shelves are filled with one copy of every single book that has ever been written. I say 'written' rather than 'published', because the moment a book is written it is automatically filed away on the appropriate shelf by your imaginary librarian.

How to Remember What You Read

When you come to use your Library of Knowledge, before you access it the first thing to do is pick up the book you want to read and weigh it in your hands. The moment you do this, your brain says, 'Oh, you're weighing the book and therefore you want to learn from it.' You flick through the book so you get an impression of what it contains. Are there any diagrams? Are there any illustrations? Is there any colour in it? What does the typeface look like? Is it a hardback or a paperback? What does the blurb on the back cover say? What do the flaps on the book jacket say? This ritual sets up the results you want. The more often you do this, the more your brain will recognize that this ritual leads on to learning from what you read. The neurones in your head will be excited and raring to go. At this stage, however, you don't yet start reading the book.

Next you pick a chapter you'd like to read. It is very important to read in the way that I call 'close-ended' – in other words, one chapter at a time. Authors write books in chapters because each chapter contains a specific block of information, and you should read them this way, too. Look at the chapter, work out how many pages it has, then look to see if it contains any diagrams or illustrations. Does the typeface change style? Is there anything particularly noticeable about the chapter? Decide how long it will take you to read this chapter at your normal reading speed. Let's say the chapter is 15 pages long, so you decide it will take you 30 minutes to read. But you still won't have started to read.

At this point, close your eyes, take three deep breaths and use the tip-of-the-tongue trigger to take you instantly into your House on the Right Bank. In your imagination picture yourself standing in your Library of Knowledge.

Imagine you are looking around at the bookshelves until you find a copy of the book you are about to read. When you spot it, take it off the shelf and sit down in the comfortable chair at your beautiful desk. State to yourself the title of the book, its author and its subject. So if you were going to read this book, you would say: 'I am looking at *MindStore for Life* by Jack Black, published by Thorsons. It will tell me how to make the most of my mental powers.' Open the book and mentally rehearse reading it. While you are pretending to yourself that you are reading the book, you are setting up the expectation in your brain of what you are about to do in reality. This mental rehearsal will take only a few seconds, yet you may find that you are so intuitively engaged in what you are doing that you will start to get impressions of the chapter's contents before you even read it. Tell yourself that you are about to read the book, mentioning the book's title, author and publisher again. 'I am about to open my eyes and while using the tip-of-the-tongue trigger I am going to read Chapter Four of Jack Black's *MindStore for Life* published by Thorsons. I will find it easy to concentrate and understand.' Then open your eyes and read while using the tip-of-the-tongue trigger. Once you finish reading the chapter, resist the temptation to turn the page and carry on. Instead, close your eyes and tell yourself 'I have now read Chapter Four of Jack Black's *MindStore for Life*. I expect to remember what I want about this chapter simply by using the tip-of-the-tongue trigger.' Then still sitting by your beautiful desk in your imagination close the book and put it back on the bookshelf. If you then want to read Chapter Five repeat the whole procedure. At the end of a session simply open your eyes and go about your business.

No one else will know that you are using the tip-of-the-tongue trigger while you read, but your brain will and, because you are reading in alpha/theta, you will remember what you read. Once you finish reading the chapter, resist the temptation to turn the page and carry on. Instead, close your eyes and tell yourself: 'I have now read Chapter Four of Jack Black's *MindStore for Life*, published by Thorsons. It tells me how to make the most of my mental powers. And I expect to remember what I want about this chapter simply by using the tip-of-the-tongue trigger.' If you then want to read Chapter Five, repeat the whole procedure.

It takes between 30 seconds and 1 minute to set up this ritual – in fact, it takes much longer to explain than to do – which isn't long at all, especially when you consider how many times you might have to read that chapter if you were using your normal methods of retaining information.

Using the Stage

Do you remember I said that there is a stage, with a few chairs in front of it, in your Library of Knowledge? This is for you to use if you have to go into a classroom or meeting, to improve the quality of your recall and also the quality of your contribution during that meeting or class.

I have noticed time and again how people lose their concentration during meetings and miss hearing or taking part in important aspects of what is going on. Someone arrives late or becomes distracted, and he or she is immediately at an immense disadvantage. I have developed a technique that ensures you the maximum level of concentration and helps you to make valuable contributions whenever you attend a meeting or class.

If you have to travel to get to the meeting, class or course (and by the way, this technique will put you at a tremendous advantage if you attend one of my MindStore courses!), the first thing you must do when you arrive at your destination is make straight for the 'alpha closet', or somewhere else that is quiet and private, and enjoy some QRT. Relax your body fully, then enter your House on the Right Bank and have a Shower. When you have finished the Shower, walk through your Central Hallway into your Library of Knowledge and sit on one of the chairs in front of the stage. Look up at the stage and imagine the meeting taking place as though it were a play. Mentally rehearse on the stage the meeting, class or course. At the same time see yourself playing an appropriate role. Tell yourself that you will appreciate and understand everything that takes place during the meeting, class or course. This is most effective if you mentally say to yourself: 'I am now going to open my eyes and participate in the meeting/class/course given on [name the date] by [name the teacher, lecturer or person who called the meeting]. I will have superior concentration and understanding, I will play an appropriate role and I will remember all of it at any time in the future simply by using the tip-of-the-tongue trigger.' During the meeting or course, use the tip-of-the-tongue trigger to increase your concentration and understanding. If you do all this, you will have phenomenal power and control, yet be calm and collected. In fact, you will be a force to be reckoned with. Remember, *it only works*.

Neuro-Linguistic Programming

When I was developing the Library of Knowledge, there was a lot of excitement about Neuro-Linguistic Programming, or NLP, because of the additional insight it gives into how the brain works. People studying NLP have discovered that when people want to access a memory or think about something visual, they turn their eyes upwards while they search for the memory. Some people do it so fast that it takes a high-speed camera to record them doing it, others do it much more slowly. Whether fast or slow, when this happens the eye goes up to what is called 'the natural visual accessing position'. It is believed that this is what triggers the electrical impulse in the brain that produces the memory.

Having accepted that, I decided to incorporate it in this technique. So when you create the lecture hall in your imagination, I want you to turn your eyes up behind your eyelids to their natural visual accessing position to find the surface of the stage. Do this too whenever you mentally rehearse a meeting or lecture, and when you want to remember it afterwards; the quality of your concentration and understanding will be immense.

I will now give you the exercise that enables you to create your Library of Knowledge. Note that it uses the tip-of-the-tongue trigger to put you instantly into your imaginary landscape of abundance. However, this does not mean you can now skip the relaxation exercise that you have been doing so far, because it is an essential part of enjoying QRT, combating stress and achieving peak performance. You will use the tip-of-the-tongue trigger whenever you need instant access to your House on the Right Bank. If you are short of time, you can immediately imagine yourself in your Library of Knowledge, but whenever possible you should imagine yourself in the landscape of abundance and enter your house through the Conditioning Gym. This ensures you do not carry any negative thoughts into your house.

EXERCISE SEVEN: THE LIBRARY OF KNOWLEDGE
Find a comfortable position in your chair, close your eyes and begin breathing slowly and regularly.

Take a deep breath and relax ... take another deep breath and relax ... take a deep breath and again relax ...

Gently touch the roof of your mouth directly behind your two front teeth with the tip of your tongue. Whenever you use the tip-of-the-tongue trigger like this, you will immediately enter your foundation level and access your faculties of concentration, imagination and intuition. The tip-of-the-tongue trigger is a powerful programming tool that you can use for whatever purpose you desire.

Take a deep breath and relax ... I will now imagine that I am standing on a river bank ... The river is behind me and I am facing a wonderful landscape ...

I can feel my feet on the lush green grass ... overhead the sky is blue and the air is fresh with the scent of the meadow ... I can hear the sounds of this wonderful land before me ...

I now look towards my house and remind myself of its construction, the features of the walls, the red roof and the entrance area ... I move forward now and into my Entrance Vestibule, past my Symbol of Potential and on into my Conditioning Gym ...

In a moment I will stand within my Shower and cleanse away any negativity and underlying thought patterns ...

I now enter my showering area and turn on the flow, so that its imaginary cleansing action can commence ... I feel the warm spring waters running down my hair and over every inch of my body, draining away mental fatigue and restoring vibrant life ...

I now imagine the bright sunlight reaching deep within ... filtering out and washing away all my limiting and destructive attitudes, particularly my negative thoughts ...

Readjusting and turning off the Shower I now step out, instantly dry, and fresh with positive expectations ...

In a moment I will create my Library of Knowledge, which

is entered by a doorway off my Central Hallway ... I am now leaving my Conditioning Gym and entering my Central Hallway ... The walls are covered with images depicting moments from my past when I have been at my very best ...

I am now creating the room that will house my Library of Knowledge ... I am choosing the size of this area and the height of the ceiling ... Now I am choosing the decorative features, the colours and the lighting ... I am now constructing the lecture hall, with a stage and a row of seats in front of it ... I am now installing my desk and chair ... I am now lining the walls with bookshelves containing the volumes of universal knowledge ...

I will now leave the house and return to the river's edge ... I feel the lush green grass beneath my feet ... Soon I will count from 1 to 7, and gradually adjust to come out of this healthy state of deep relaxation ...

1 ... 2 ... 3 ... 4 ... now, beyond the midpoint, when I open my eyes I will be wide awake and revitalized both physically and mentally ... 5, I begin to adjust my body ... 6, I prepare to open my eyes ... and 7, I open my eyes and am wide awake now, both physically and mentally alert.

Using Mind Maps

If you use the techniques I have just described, you will put yourself in a very strong position. However, taking notes while at a meeting or course gives you even more of an advantage. Next time you attend a meeting with your colleagues and they do not take notes, you will realize that they are only half-engaged in what is going on. If you take notes as well as listen (using the tip-of-the-tongue trigger all the while), you will be doubly engaged in the meeting and you will learn more and get more out of it.

When it comes to taking notes, many of us are caught up in old strategies. For instance, most people take written notes on lined paper. In fact it's quite a feat finding any notebooks or pads that don't have lined paper, but that's exactly what you are going to look for from now on. And the bigger the better, because you will need all the space you can get for the new way you will make notes. Some people say they don't take notes because there is too much to write down. However, a technique called Mind Maps provides the solution.

Mind Maps were the brainwave of Tony Buzan, and I have been using them for a good 20 years. Instead of the usual written notes that people take, which only use the left side of the brain, Mind Maps use both sides of the brain and also reflect the brain's natural way of processing information. They use keywords and trigger words, saving you time because you do not have to add screeds of extraneous information; you can also use quick drawings. Because Mind Maps operate in the same way as your brain's recall system, you will be able to remember what each of these keywords and drawings means when you go over your notes later. You will also remember everything that was said relating to each topic. In fact, I have some Mind Maps that are over 10 years old and I can still remember and understand them. You can also use Mind Maps when planning ideas and concepts. I planned this book with one big Mind Map, then each chapter was given its own Mind Map so I could organize my thoughts quickly and logically.

If you want to learn about Mind Maps in more detail, and I strongly urge you to do so, read Tony Buzan's groundbreaking book *Use Your Head*. In the meantime, here is a brief outline of what you do.

- Turn a blank sheet of unlined A4 paper (or, even better, A3 paper) on its side so that it is wider than it is long ('landscape'). Using coloured pens or pencils (not just blue or black), write the name of the subject in the middle of the paper, surrounded if possible by a drawing that symbolizes that subject.
- Draw thick lines radiating out from this centre drawing to represent the main aspects of the subject. Develop each aspect by drawing more lines that radiate out from the main line.
- Label each line in block capitals with the keyword that sums up that particular idea. Choose keywords that are creative and associative (strong nouns or verbs are usually best).
- Whenever possible, use a different colour for each main line. Use drawings and illustrations, too, as these help to trigger your creative thought processes.

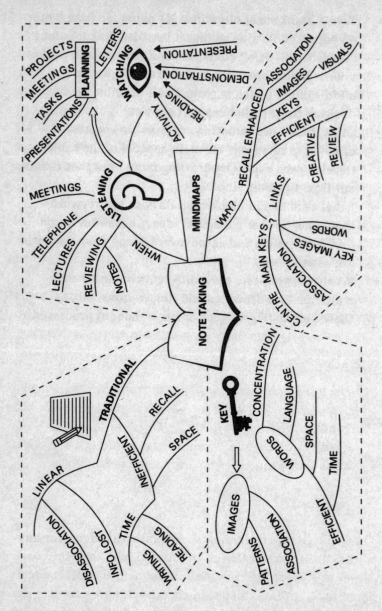

Mind Mapping

Please be brave about using Mind Maps. Your comfort zones may be severely challenged by them at first, and you may wonder what your colleagues will say when you get out a pad of A3 paper and a box of coloured felt-tip pens at your next meeting. To help you with this, focus on the benefits that Mind Maps will bring you. I am sure that, before very long, you will have made such remarkable progress that all your colleagues will want to keep pace with you and will also start to use Mind Maps. Who knows, you may have to hold your meetings at larger tables from now on!

Exam Techniques

One of the big challenges for any student is how he or she deals with exams. Sometimes the success or otherwise of a whole course rests on how a student fares in exams. Exams can cause tremendous anxiety, negativity and self-doubt. However, if you use the techniques I am about to describe, you need never feel challenged by the thought of exams again. You may even start to look forward to them!

The following techniques were developed out of a workshop I ran many years ago for people sitting exams. About 70 people turned up, from young children to mature students, and everyone shared his or her experience of exams. The ideas that emerged were absolutely fascinating.

Keep Away!

The children especially had some fantastic advice for anyone taking an exam. One of the first things they said was, 'Never to go near the examination room until the last possible minute.' In fact, they said you shouldn't even enter the building where the exam is taking place until you absolutely have to. Sit in your car, in your mother's car or on a park bench for as long as possible, or disappear into the 'alpha closet' and keep out of the way.

There is a very good reason for this. If you take your mind back to your school days, you will remember how you felt before an exam: the high level of anxiety and your friends wailing, 'I know I'm going to fail, I'm lousy at exams' making you think 'Oh, no! I'm lousy at them, too.' And do you remember the brainy ones saying, 'I know I'm going to fail because I haven't revised a thing' even though you knew they'd done nothing else for weeks? If you recall how all that felt you will understand why you should keep your distance until the last minute. Otherwise, your brain will listen to all that negative energy and will process it, especially if you find yourself joining in with a statement like, 'I haven't revised, either.' Your brain won't know whether you are telling the truth or not, it will simply process your thought.

Choosing the Best Seat

When it is time to enter the building, or to emerge from the alpha closet, do so with your protective glass screen in place. When you walk into the exam room, if possible sit next to the students you know will pass, so you can benefit from their positive energy fields. Who knows, some of their answers may even float over in your direction! If your seat has been allocated to you already and you are sitting next to people who seem sure they'll fail, make sure your glass screen is firmly in position; you don't want to absorb their negative energies.

Reading the Exam Paper

When the exam starts, you are always told to turn over the exam paper and start reading the questions. Do you remember how that felt? You would start reading and your brain, which had probably listened to weeks of negative self-talk such as, 'I know I can't do it' or 'I'm useless at this subject' would start to obey the instructions you had been giving it. After all, your subconscious can do many things, but the one thing it can't do is take a joke. So even if you say jokingly that you don't stand a chance in a forthcoming exam, your subconscious brain will take note of what you said. It won't hear the laughter that follows it, it will simply hear your words.

So, let's say you start reading the exam questions. The first question is easy, you can answer it and you put a tick against it on the exam paper. The same goes for question two, and you start to feel better. Maybe this won't be so bad after all. You read on. You know the answers to questions three, four and five. But you don't know the answer to question six. And, oh my goodness, you don't know the answer to question seven either. All that negative self-talk comes flooding back – 'I knew I was going to fail, I don't know how to do this.' You carry on reading, and you can answer questions eight, nine and ten. That means you have the potential to gain an 80 per cent pass, but you will probably focus on the two questions you can't answer rather than the eight that you can.

The children at the workshop told us that you should read exam questions in a different way. They said to read the first question and, if you can answer it, to jot down your answer immediately in the form of a Mind Map. It only takes a couple of minutes and it gives you a big psychological advantage. Read question two and, if you can answer it, jot down another Mind Map. Carry on in this way through the exam paper. If you come across a question you can't answer, use MindStore's F-word – 'Fantastic!' You feel optimistic. You think of the way the subconscious brain works and feel confident that, while you are answering the other questions, it will be sifting away through your memory looking for the answer. Maybe you draw a blank over the next question too, so you say 'Fantastic!' again. When you have finished reading the exam paper, you will have Mind Maps for each of the questions you can answer, and can start turning these into written answers.

Only when you have finished all these answers do you turn again to the questions that you couldn't answer immediately. You read the first one again, and now the answer falls into your mind. Your subconscious has done the trick, so you jot down a Mind Map. Then you read the other question, but still you can't recall the answer. Go back to the first one, and turn the Mind Map into a proper written answer. If the second one is still out of reach, you have two choices, both calling for the tip-of-the-tongue trigger and your Library of Knowledge.

- Imagine you are sitting in one of the seats in your lecture hall. Pretend your teacher or lecturer is standing on the stage, smiling at you. In your imagination, ask him or her the question for which you need an answer. Listen carefully to the reply and don't let your logic get in the way.
- Alternatively, you can enter your Library of Knowledge and imagine that you are taking down from your bookshelves the book that contains the answer you are looking for. Open the book, find the relevant page and read what it says.

Keeping your tongue behind your teeth, jot down the answer you were given in the form of a Mind Map.

Remember what Einstein said: 'Imagination is more important than knowledge.' Clearly you only use this imaginative and intuitive technique if you have no other way of knowing the answer. You will feel like you are making it up; you won't know for certain that it's correct and your logic will want to get involved. But trust your imagination and hand in your paper.

Learning to Fly

I have heard some amazing stories from MindStore members who have used these techniques in exams. A 16-year-old girl told me she'd got the top grade for her GCSE-level English – that's great for anyone, but this girl happens to be dyslexic. She said that during the exam she imagined her teacher standing beside her. She asked the teacher all the exam questions and the teacher told her the answers.

It's a magnificent, wonderful story, and the joy of it is that you can also achieve the same fantastic results if you use these techniques. Yes, people will always be challenged by them, for a number of reasons which will probably include envy, but if you are willing to cope with that and you really want to succeed, you will.

5

Habits

How many times have you told yourself that you are going to stop eating chocolate biscuits with your afternoon cup of tea, give up smoking, write that novel you've always talked about, or do any of the other things you are always putting off? And how many times have you still not done them? Most of us, if we are honest, would have to admit that it's happened to us, too. We tell ourselves that we'll start tomorrow but, as the saying goes, tomorrow never comes.

In this chapter I will show you how to seize control of the habits that rule your life and that you want to change. Please note that I said '*want* to change'. If you feel that you ought to stop smoking, cut down on your drinking or whatever, but your heart isn't really in it, the techniques in this chapter will not work for you. As I explained in Chapter Four, you must have the *desire* to make changes in your life. If you don't have that desire, you will not succeed.

Challenging Our Comfort Zones

In Chapter 1 I talked about how everyone has comfort zones relating to every aspect of life. In other words, most of us have areas within which we feel safe and which we are reluctant to move out of. I have them about being a father, being a team leader, being a friend, being a husband, being a Scotsman, being a golfer, everything. I don't drink a lot of alcohol, but I do love malt whisky and I have a comfort zone about it. If my doctor were to tell me to give up whisky and start drinking an infusion of lawn-clippings instead, my comfort zone would be severely challenged by the prospect. (So would my stomach, but that's another matter.) I might think 'Fantastic, I can't wait to start,' but I would be more likely to think 'You must be joking!', check that he had a good reason for his suggestion and, if he hadn't, immediately change doctors. I would only switch to drinking infused lawn-clippings if it was absolutely essential.

Most of us feel the same way about any habit that we have to break. The big challenge is to allow your comfort zones to grow in whichever way you need. As you might expect, there is a MindStore technique to enable you to do this.

Get into the Groove

Constant repetition of a particular habit turns it into part of your subconscious. Let's pretend that you always have a big piece of fruit cake and a cup of tea at four in the afternoon, every day, come summer or winter. Because this happens every day, the thinking process that tells you it is ten to four and time to put the kettle on has worn a groove in your brain. You now associate 'ten to four' with teatime. If you want to break this association, you must find a way of filling in that groove and creating a new one that does not include having cake and tea every day. This chapter will teach you how to do that, in order to conquer any habit that you want to break.

Giving Up Smoking

This is a tough one for many, many people. They know their health would be better if they gave up cigarettes, they know they would have more money in their pockets, they know their doctors would stop nagging them about the alarming things that cigarettes can do to their bodies. Yet they still smoke. In fact, they may even smoke more through sheer worry about it.

There are many ways of finding help in giving up cigarettes, including hypnotism and those nicotine patches you can wear. I heard of a man who went to a hypnotist for help in stopping smoking. The first session was great. Afterwards, this guy was able to walk past tobacconists without a second thought; he was able to counter the cravings. This was easy! The following week he went back to his hypnotist for the second session and again came out feeling great. So he went to the pub to celebrate. There he was, drinking his beer, when he glanced up and saw his hypnotist standing by the bar. And guess what the hypnotist was doing? He was smoking! That was the end of this guy's cure; he nearly broke the sound barrier in his rush to the cigarette machine.

I have also heard of people's experiences with those nicotine chewing gums and patches. I even know of one woman who used the patches *and* carried on smoking! She said it meant the cigarettes gave her an even bigger buzz than usual.

The MindStore technique for giving up smoking doesn't require nicotine patches, nicotine gum or anything else. All it requires is your heartfelt desire to make this change in your life. Your subconscious will do the rest.

- Choose a time in your day when you won't be interrupted, sit comfortably in your chair and use the Standard Entry Exercise to enter your House on the Right Bank. Now enter your Editing Suite. Programme the date at the top of the screen, then insert a video cassette in the video machine. Use the remote-control handset to create an image of yourself smoking on your central screen.
- Using your remote-control handset, look at your past screen. Study when you first started to smoke, why you did it and what you like about it.
- Turn back to your central screen. Admit and accept the image of you smoking. Now, with the remote-control handset, reduce the size, colour and sound of the image until it is a tiny dot on the screen. Press the Delete button on your handset and erase the image of you smoking for ever.
- Now, using your remote-control handset, turn to your future screen. Imagine that you are looking at a day-to-a-page diary. Turn over the pages until you come to the page for 30 days from today. Imagine you are writing on this page 'On this day I will stop smoking and never use cigarettes again in my life.' Use the remote-control handset to enlarge the size, sound and sensations of this image until it is huge, then freeze-frame it and surround it with brilliant white light.
- You have now programmed that you will stop smoking. Using the tip-of-the-tongue trigger, visit your Editing

Suite every night and every morning and look at the freeze-framed page in the diary. Each time you have a cigarette, remind yourself that you will give up smoking on the date you have chosen. You will either stop smoking gradually or you will continue smoking until you wake up on that date and stop then. Either way, you will never smoke again.

Giving Up Chocolate

You can use exactly the same technique to give up chocolate or, for that matter, any other habit connected with food or drink. Use it to stop drinking, give up coffee, give up tea, stop taking recreational drugs, kick your custard-tart habit or give up anything else that is presenting a challenge to your health or your waistline.

One friend of mine was addicted to heroin. It was slowly destroying his health and his life, yet he carried on being a junkie. However, he kicked the habit for ever when he used this technique.

Controlling Your Weight

In many countries of the developed world, obesity is presenting an enormous challenge. What's more, the number of people who are seriously overweight or obese is growing each year. Clearly, something needs to be done to stop this trend. I will discuss how making simple changes to your diet can improve your health and help you to lose weight in Chapter Eight, but in this chapter I want to give you a simple technique that will enable you to lose weight quickly, using the power of your subconscious.

- Choose a time in your day when you won't be interrupted, sit comfortably in your chair and use the Standard Entry Exercise to enter your House on the Right Bank. Now enter your Editing Suite. Programme the date at the top of the screen, then insert a video cassette in the video machine.
- Use the remote-control handset to create an image of yourself as you weigh and look now on your central screen. Accept your current appearance.
- Turn to the past screen and use the remote-control handset to rewind and play back the events and habits that have contributed to the way you look now.
- Return to the central screen, then reduce the image of yourself until it is a tiny dot. Press the Delete button on your handset to erase the image for ever.
- Turn to the future screen and create an image of the way you want to look. Concentrate on getting the details right. Then see yourself standing on a set of scales which displays your ideal weight.
- Play the scene forward and see yourself going into a clothes shop. Imagine asking the assistant who comes forward to bring you some clothing in your new, ideal size. See yourself trying it on and looking fantastic in it.
- Play another scene in which your family and friends are complimenting you on your wonderful appearance. Listen to their compliments and encouraging words. Feel terrific at what you are hearing. Programme the date for when you want this to happen.
- Use your remote-control handset to adjust the sound, size and brightness of the image. Make it as big as possible, then freeze-frame it in brilliant white light.

You have now created your future history, and you know that it exists. From now on, whenever you think of your weight or food, use the tip-of-the-tongue trigger to call up the image of your future history. Pretend and act as if you have already achieved your desired weight, and know that it will happen.

People Who Succeed Take Action

I am often asked what I think makes a successful person. I always reply that a successful person is one who is good at solving problems. People who are successful face just as many challenges as everyone else, but they are better at resolving them. You need only think of phenomenally successful people such as Richard Branson, Anita Roddick and Bill Gates to appreciate the number of challenges they face every day. But can you imagine any one of them indulging in procrastination, telling themselves that they'll launch that new product next week because they can't be bothered right now, or postponing that meeting they aren't looking forward to? Instead, they seize the day by taking action.

You can do the same. If you are one of the many people who would like to stop being a procrastinator but can't quite get round to it, you will know that delaying things can put you under an enormous amount of strain. In fact, it usually puts you under more strain than if you were to grit your teeth and tackle the thing you are putting off. You may feel guilt, worry, self-doubt, frustration and fatigue. When you finally stop putting something off and get on with it, you usually find it isn't nearly as difficult as you had thought. What's more, you experience a wave of relief that it's finally done, and probably feel that a weight has been lifted from your shoulders.

If you want to avoid putting the weight there in the first

place and save your energy for something positive, you need to take action to eradicate procrastination from your life. The following simple MindStore technique can help.

- Choose a time in your day when you won't be interrupted, sit comfortably in your chair and use the Standard Entry Exercise to enter your House on the Right Bank. Now enter your Editing Suite. Programme the date at the top of the screen, then insert a video cassette in the video machine.
- Use your remote-control handset to create an image on your central screen of whatever it is you are putting off.
- Turn to the past screen to make a good study of the previous times when you have procrastinated. Explore the reasons for this.
- Return to the central screen and ask yourself why you are procrastinating at the moment. Is it because the task you are facing is unpleasant, time-consuming or threatening? Are you being a perfectionist and putting it off until the conditions are just right? Are you resisting change or focusing on ineffective goals? Ask yourself if you are secretly frightened, either of being a success or a failure.
- Use your remote-control handset to turn down the size and sound of, and the emotions you associate with, this image. Reduce it to a tiny dot and erase it for ever.
- Turn to your future screen and see yourself starting to tackle the task you have been putting off. Play the scene forward and see yourself completing it. Programme the date for when you want this to happen. Use the handset to turn up the size, sounds and emotions of this image, then freeze-frame it and surround it with brilliant white light.

You have now created your future history, and you know that it exists. For more help in tackling your task, follow these steps:

- Divide up any large tasks into more manageable units. Set target dates for achieving each one. Do this on your future screen.
- Organize your tasks according to their priority. Get started on the most important or pressing tasks now. That means today!
- Inform the people who can offer support of what you are about to do, and tell them when and what you will achieve.
- Choose a reward that you will give yourself only if you complete the task in full and on time.
- If you find yourself procrastinating in the meantime, review your future history using the tip-of-the-tongue trigger and, if necessary, give yourself a pep talk.

Getting a Good Night's Sleep

Are you a good sleeper? Do you fall asleep the moment your head hits the pillow each night, or does it take you ages to drop off? Does your mind fill with negative, worrying thoughts? Perhaps your sleep patterns vary, so that sometimes you sleep like a baby all through the night and other times you wake in the early hours and can't get back to sleep because your mind starts racing. That used to happen to me a lot. I would wake up in the middle of the night, look at my alarm clock and think, 'Oh, no, I'll never get back to sleep now' and, sure enough, I wouldn't. And that was the cue for my mind to go into overdrive, worrying about everything it possibly could. If I ever did manage to go back to sleep, it would be a fitful, uneasy sleep and I would wake in the morning feeling tired and listless.

If any of this sounds familiar, the following technique will enable you to establish a different, positive sleeping pattern for the rest of your life.

The last thoughts of the day are the most important. It is a time when big ideas can come, as I will explain in the next chapter; but it is also a time when big worries can strike. The reason for this is simple. Let's say you've had a busy day and you've spent the evening watching TV. You can hardly keep your eyes open, so you totter into bed and start to doze off. As you move towards sleep, your brain starts to produce alpha rhythms but, instead of gently drifting off to sleep, your right brain is triggered. Maybe it hasn't had a look-in all day and it's been waiting to feed you ideas, but they turn out to be negative ones. Perhaps you suddenly remember that you still haven't paid the phone bill. Oh, no, will you get cut off? How will you find the money to pay it? And you're off! In comes the adrenalin because you are feeling stressed, back come the beta-frequency brain waves, out come the worries, and away goes any chance of sleep. You've just set yourself up for a night of tossing and turning. You have also programmed a negative future for yourself because all your thoughts about what you will do tomorrow or the next day are gloom-filled ones.

The Importance of Good-quality Sleep

On average, we spend one-third of our lives asleep. That means a 60-year-old has spent 20 of his or her years tucked up in bed, fast asleep. No wonder it is so important to have good-quality sleep. But what do you do if you have fallen into a pattern of spending ages getting to sleep every night or waking up in the early hours and then lying there, wide awake and feeling frustrated?

Sleep is vital to your well-being. A good night's sleep sets you up for the day ahead, gives you a long stretch of rest, and enables your body to repair itself. Most of us can cope when we have the odd night of broken sleep, but functioning properly during the day can be a real challenge when you have had a string of wakeful nights, your limbs are heavy and you feel as if you can't keep your eyes open. That is why I developed the following techniques, to ensure that from now on you will sleep better than ever before.

Alarm Clocks are Alarming

Alarm clocks are aptly named. If you are already awake when your alarm clock goes off, you will probably find the noise irritating or intrusive. If you are still asleep, it will rudely jerk you awake and your first reaction of the day will be one of shock. Not the best start to the day, is it?

Zig Zigler, eminent in the field of personal development, has renamed the alarm clock 'the opportunity clock'. He associates it with the fantastic opportunities and openings that the coming day will bring. I am going to show you how to dispense with your real-life alarm clock for ever, replacing it with your own Opportunity Clock in your subconscious.

If you currently use an ordinary alarm, most mornings you probably wake up just before it goes off anyway (that is certainly true of many of the people who attend the Mind-Store courses). That happens because you are not daft. You would rather wake up *before* the alarm sounds than be jolted out of a warm, relaxing sleep. After all, who wants a shock first thing in the morning? That's another reason for never using an alarm clock again – it might interrupt a significant or enjoyable dream you are having, so that you wake up feeling frustrated or wanting to know what happened next. Neither of these is a good way to welcome the new day.

If you are always giving yourself another five minutes before you have to get out of bed in the morning, setting your Opportunity Clock will make an enormous difference to your energy levels. Your sleep cycles will automatically adjust to ensure that the last cycle of the night ends just at the time you have programmed, so you will wake feeling refreshed and raring to go, rather than bleary-eyed and muggy-headed.

The Sleeping Quarters

I am going to teach you how to create a bedroom in your House on the Right Bank. You will sleep in this room for the rest of your life, and the quality of your sleep may well be better than any you have experienced before.

You will construct your Sleeping Quarters in one of the rooms leading off your Central Hallway. Taking up all the space on one wall will be a huge clock face – this will be your Opportunity Clock. You can choose a digital or analogue clock, but from now on you will use this clock to wake you up in the mornings, *not* your alarm clock.

Somewhere else in the room will be a wonderfully relaxing, comfortable bed. In your imagination you will associate this bed with deep, relaxing, replenishing sleep. You can imagine a bed that you have actually slept in, perhaps as a child or recently on holiday, or you can create your own design. Be as adventurous as you like – it can even be a bed of roses, if that's what you want.

When you go to bed at night – and why not start using

this technique tonight? – and are ready for sleep, sit up in bed with your pillows propped behind you. I realize that when you are ready to sleep you normally lie down, but it is important to sit up in bed the first few times you do this exercise, because if you do it lying down you will probably become so relaxed that you will fall asleep halfway through. Most people do not fall asleep sitting upright (unless they have had a few drinks), so your brain will notice what is going on and think 'Aha, this is different.' After you have mastered this technique sitting up, you will be able to do it easily lying down.

Setting the Opportunity Clock

So sit up, close your eyes, take three deep breaths and relax your body from head to toe. If your brain is buzzing with thoughts, take yourself off to your favourite place of relaxation and, if you wish, count down from 100 to 1 or from Z to A. Otherwise, go through the Standard Entry Exercise until you have finished your Shower. Walk along your Central Hallway, looking at the fantastic images on the walls, enter your Sleeping Quarters and sit on the bed so you face the clock. This will be telling the real time. Don't open your eyes to check you've got the time absolutely correct, simply trust your instincts that you've got it roughly right.

Now imagine that the hands or numbers on the clock are moving rapidly forward, just as they do in the movies to signify the passing of time. Watch the hours passing until the clock stops at exactly the time you want to wake up the following morning. If you are one of those people whose visual imagination could be better, use your audio or kinaesthetic thinking powers instead. Hear the clock's hands clicking as they pass each hour, or imagine yourself physically turning them. When you have set your clock, tell yourself that this is the time you will wake up. Because your brain is in alpha/theta, it will listen to what you have told it and obey.

If you really want to master MindStore and make it work for you, you have to trust in this clock. If you are unable to change the simple things in your life such as your alarm clock, you will not be able to change the big things. By the way, it is no good setting your real alarm for the same time, or for 15 minutes later, just in case, because your subconscious will know that it doesn't have to wake you up at the right time and it won't bother. So from now on, use the clock or watch by your bed for time-keeping only; never again set that alarm.

I realize that it won't be easy at first to trust that this technique will work, but once you get used to the idea it will never let you down. Believe me, *it only works*.

If you wake up long before your Opportunity Clock is set to go off, all you need do is reset it and go back to sleep. If you wake up only half an hour or so before you wanted to, you can tell yourself that you have obviously slept for long enough so you might as well get up and do something enjoyable, such as read a book or write a letter. I do this a lot, and whenever I reach the point when I think it is time to put the book down or stop writing, it is always exactly the time that I programmed myself to wake up.

I am sure you would agree that not everyone needs eight hours' sleep every night. Some people need more, others considerably less. Your sleep patterns may also be seasonal, as I expect you have noticed in your own life. I often wake up early in the summer, say at half-past four, and decide to get up. It looks so gorgeous out there that I can't bear to stay in bed and miss it all. Besides, it is only our luggage of life that says 'It's half-past four and I'm wide awake, but I never get up until seven.' Your body is awake, so enjoy it. The world is a fantastic place when you've got it all to yourself, and early summer mornings in particular are magnificent. Listen to the birds, do some light gardening, go for a walk while there is hardly any traffic on the roads – it's the best time of day.

The Pathway to Sleep

Once you have set your Opportunity Clock, open your eyes just long enough to slide into your favourite sleeping position and get nice and comfortable, then close your eyes again so you are back in alpha/theta. In your imagination, climb into the large, comfortable bed in your Sleeping Quarters. Now, start to relax your body. Concentrate on relaxing your scalp, then say, 'I'm falling into a deep, relaxing sleep now.' Repeat this five times, then start to concentrate on relaxing your forehead, repeating the phrase another five times. Then move on to your eyelids, and so on down your body.

Sooner or later (usually sooner), you will fall into a deep, deep sleep because you will find this relaxation process so boring. In fact, it's unbelievably boring, and after a couple of minutes of it your brain will be saying 'For goodness sake, let's go to sleep!' And that is exactly what will happen.

EXERCISE EIGHT: THE SLEEPING QUARTERS

Find a comfortable position in your chair, close your eyes and begin breathing in a regular and slow manner. You will now begin to focus your mind and body on relaxing into a healthy state of being. Once again, as each part of your body is mentioned, concentrate on it and focus your thinking on producing relaxation.

Take a deep breath and relax ... take another deep breath and relax ... take a deep breath and again relax ... My scalp is relaxed, I feel my scalp relaxed ... My forehead is relaxed, I feel my forehead relaxed ... My eyelids are relaxed, I feel my eyelids relaxed ... My face is relaxed, I feel my face relaxed ... My tongue is relaxed, I feel my tongue relaxed ... My jaw is relaxed, I feel my jaw relaxed ... My throat is relaxed, I feel my throat relaxed ...

My shoulders are relaxed, I feel my shoulders relaxed ... My arms and hands are relaxed, I feel my arms and hands relaxed ... My upper back is relaxed, I feel my upper back relaxed ... My chest is relaxed, I feel my chest relaxed ... My lower back is relaxed, I feel my lower back relaxed ...

My abdomen is relaxed, I feel my abdomen relaxed ... My hips are relaxed, I feel my hips relaxed ... My thighs are relaxed, I feel my thighs relaxed ... My knees are relaxed, I feel my knees relaxed ... My calves are relaxed, I feel my calves relaxed ... My ankles are relaxed, I feel my ankles relaxed ... My toes are relaxed, I feel my toes relaxed ... My soles are relaxed, I feel my soles relaxed ... My heels are relaxed, I feel my heels relaxed ...

Take a deep breath and relax ... I will now imagine that I am in a very special place of relaxation ... I am there ... I will give myself a short period to enjoy this fully [pause for approx. 20 to 30 seconds] ...

Once again I take a deep breath and relax ... I will now adjust and imagine that I am standing on a river bank ... The river is behind me and I am facing a wonderful landscape ...

I can feel my feet on the lush green grass ... overhead the sky is blue and the air is fresh with the scent of the meadow ... I can hear the sounds of this wonderful land before me ...

I now move forward and through the doorway of my house with the red roof ... into my Entrance Vestibule, past my Symbol of Potential and on into my Conditioning Gym ...

In a moment I will stand within my Shower and cleanse away any negativity and underlying thought patterns ...

I now enter my showering area and turn on the flow so that its imaginary cleansing action can commence ... I feel the warm spring waters running down my hair and over every inch of my body, draining away mental fatigue and restoring vibrant life ...

I now imagine the bright sunlight reaching deep within ... filtering out and washing away all my limiting and destructive attitudes, particularly my negative thoughts ...

Readjusting and turning off the Shower I now step out, instantly dry, and fresh with positive expectations ...

In a moment I will create my Sleeping Quarters, which are entered by a doorway off my Central Hallway ... They will be used for sleeping soundly and developing my creativity ...

I now leave my Conditioning Gym and enter my Central Hallway ... the walls are covered with images depicting times from my past when I have been at my very best ... I now create the room that will house my Sleeping Quarters ... I decide on its shape, the height of the ceiling ... now the decorative features, colours and lighting ... On one of the walls I place an attractive clock face that covers the entire wall ... And now a large, comfortable bed ...

By entering my House on the Right Bank last thing at night and setting the time at which I wish to wake up on the clock face, and by falling asleep by the Pathway to Sleep, I will fall into a deep, relaxing sleep before waking up on time, feeling wonderful and in perfect health ...

I have now created my Sleeping Quarters for sleeping soundly and developing my creativity ...

I will now leave the house and return to the river's edge ... I feel the lush green grass beneath my feet ... Soon I will count from 1 to 7, and gradually adjust to come out of this healthy state of deep relaxation ...

1 ... 2 ... 3 ... 4 ... now, beyond the midpoint, when I open my eyes I will be wide awake and revitalized both physically and mentally ... 5, I begin to adjust my body ... 6, I prepare to open my eyes ... and 7, I open my eyes and am wide awake now, both physically and mentally alert.

6

Using Your Intuition

Intuition is the master skill, and an essential part of the MindStore techniques. Almost without exception, the major business gurus are saying that using your intuition is the key to a successful future. People like Richard Branson and Anita Roddick talk a lot about how their intuition works for them. And it is not only important in the business world: intuition is vital in every area of your life.

But how do you develop it? Let me assure you that if you have read this far and have started to practise the exercises in this book, you are already using your intuition. Controlling your imagination while your mind is in alpha/theta means you are using your intuition. If you think back over some of the stories I have recounted so far, you will realize that each one of them describes how someone's intuition worked for him or her.

Letting Your Intuition Flow

The big challenge for anyone when starting to use intuition is the question of whether or not it can be trusted. I know exactly how this feels, because I was just the same when I started using personal development techniques. I learned to trust that the techniques would work, and they did. And that is what you must do.

For most of us, the greatest challenge to our intuition – which is really the voice of the right brain – is the logical, rational, reasoning voice of the left brain. This is the voice that says, 'I'm not sure about this. What makes you think you're right? How do you know? Maybe you've got it wrong and you should think again?' From the moment you start to use the MindStore techniques, you must learn to blank out this voice. Say mentally to yourself, 'Delete that programme' every time you tell yourself that something won't or can't work. Trust yourself, trust that your intuition will work for you, and remember that the more you practise, the better you will get and the more confident you will be.

The Importance of Intuition

Have you ever made a split-second decision to walk down a particular street, let one train go by and wait for the next one, or avoid a certain area? If later on you had reason to be very thankful that you made that instant decision, you will know how important your intuition can be. And if you were asked why you followed your instincts, you probably said, 'Something made me walk in there' or even 'I just knew I shouldn't get on that plane; I had a bad feeling about it.'

Intuition can certainly save lives. We have all watched movies where the hero or heroine suddenly stands stock still, says 'Something's wrong with Sandy, I just know it,' leaps in his or her car and speeds off to the rescue just in the nick of time. Whenever a disaster occurs, such as a plane being hijacked or a train being involved in a crash, there will always be those who are thankful that they listened to their intuition and decided at the last moment not to make that journey.

In this chapter I want to teach you several techniques that will enable you to harness your intuition and make it work for you in all areas of your life. As I have already explained, all the MindStore techniques revolve around the use of your intuition, but here are some tools that will help you to make both instant and long-term decisions, to use the time when you are asleep to solve problems, and to make the most of your dreams.

How to Make Fast Decisions

How often have you stood in a shop, unable to decide what to buy? It happens to many of us whenever we want to buy someone a present but aren't sure of what to get. You may even stand in front of your wardrobe in the morning and think, 'I don't know what to wear!' It can be the same in a restaurant as you study the menu with increasing desperation while the waiter looks impatient and your friends urge you to hurry up and make a decision. You just can't bring yourself to choose.

If any of this sounds familiar, there are three simple tools that will allow your intuition to give you an instant answer. Each one is designed for a particular way of thinking, whether visual, audio or kinaesthetic. If you know in which way you think most often, choose that decision-making process. If you aren't sure, test out each technique and follow the one that you are most happy with. If you want to find out more about visual, audio and kinaesthetic thinking, I can recommend the book *Unlimited Power* by Anthony Robins (Simon & Schuster, 1986).

Visual Decision-making

Next time you need to make an instant decision, try this technique. Concentrate on whatever it is you want to make a decision about, then close your eyes. Place the tip of your tongue gently on the roof of your mouth behind your two front teeth, and imagine you are looking at a big set of traffic lights. Unlike most sets of traffic lights, this one has only red and green lights – no amber. Ask yourself a suitable question, such as 'Should I buy this jacket?' Look to see which traffic light comes on. If it is green, the answer is yes. If it is red, the answer is no. Trust whichever answer comes to you.

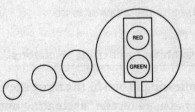

Audio Decision-making

If you tend to think mostly in an audio way, concentrate on whatever you want to make a decision about, then close your eyes, use the tip-of-the-tongue trigger and ask a question to which the answer can only be yes or no. Listen to which answer you hear in your head – and trust it.

Kinaesthetic Decision-making

Let's say you are standing in a bookshop, undecided about which of two books to buy. They both cover the same subject but you have only got enough money to buy one, so which should it be? Decide which of your hands is the stronger – if you are right-handed then your right hand will most likely be the stronger. Pick up one of the books and hold it in your stronger hand, then ask yourself if you should buy it. Wait until you feel a warm or cool feeling in this hand. Warmth indicates the answer is yes, you should buy the book; coolness means the answer is no.

How to Make Important Decisions

The following is one of the most exciting MindStore ideas of all. It is based on the fascinating and inspiring book *Think and Grow Rich* by Napoleon Hill, which is the bible for all people working in the field of personal development.

Think and Grow Rich is a book that contains the results of Napoleon Hill's interviews with 504 successful men. Andrew Carnegie commissioned him to write it because he wanted the book to convey the secrets of success to others so they could become successful too. The interviews took Napoleon 20 years to conduct, and the resulting book has sold several million copies. The whole book is phenomenal, but one part that really astonished me described Andrew Carnegie's imaginary board of directors. Each night, when he was about to fall asleep, he would imagine he was in a room with a big boardroom table. Around that table were seated some of the people who really inspired him. Carnegie was the chairman, the other people were the directors. Each night Carnegie would discuss his business plans with these directors, listen to what they had to say, and ask their advice. And he would act upon it. It worked phenomenally well. In fact, having an imaginary board of directors was the biggest secret of success in the book.

Napoleon Hill decided to try it for himself, using a council of nine famous people including Abraham Lincoln, Thomas Edison, Henry Ford and Charles Darwin. And it worked for Hill, too. When I read that, I knew I had to do the same thing. And now I want to teach you to do it, too.

Creating Your Board of Directors

I started off with two directors, a man and a woman; I'd suggest you do the same. Spend a couple of minutes thinking about whom you would like to choose for your two directors. You can choose someone famous from the past or present, someone you really admire in your personal life, a character from a novel or film, or anyone else who comes to mind. Trust your instincts about the people you think of. If you can't think of anyone at the moment, wait and see who arrives.

People who have done this on the courses sometimes tell me that surprising people become their directors. One guy told me that he felt very challenged by his choice of a woman director, because the one he had thought of failed to appear in his imagination when he did the exercise. A very famous woman television presenter arrived instead – someone he couldn't abide! Yet he kept her on because he trusted his intuition, and he told me that her advice had helped him enormously. So keep an open mind, and don't be surprised at what happens!

In the following exercise you will use the tip-of-the-tongue trigger to put you into your landscape of abundance. Then you will enter your House on the Right Bank, have a Shower and create the Boardroom. When you next do the exercise, you will welcome in your male director, followed by your female director, then you will have a short conversation with them. You will feel you are making up this conversation, but that is the right feeling to have, so trust what you are doing. Your controlled imagination will be driven by your intuition.

EXERCISE NINE: THE BOARDROOM
Find a comfortable position in your chair, close your eyes and begin breathing slowly and regularly.

Take a deep breath and relax ... take another deep breath and relax ... take a deep breath and again relax ...

Gently touch the roof of your mouth directly behind your two front teeth with the tip of your tongue. Whenever you use the tip-of-the-tongue trigger like this, you will immediately enter your foundation level and access your faculties of concentration, imagination and intuition. The tip-of-the-tongue trigger is a powerful programming tool that you can use for whatever purpose you desire.

Take a deep breath and relax ... I will now imagine that I am standing on a river bank ... The river is behind me and I am facing a wonderful landscape ...

I can feel my feet on the lush green grass ... overhead the sky is blue and the air is fresh with the scent of the meadow ... I can hear the sounds of this wonderful land before me ...

I now look towards my house and remind myself of its construction, the features of the walls, the red roof and the entrance area ... I move forward now and into my Entrance Vestibule, past my Symbol of Potential and on into my Conditioning Gym ...

In a moment I will stand within my Shower and cleanse away any negativity and underlying thought patterns ...

I now enter my showering area and turn on the flow, so that its imaginary cleansing action can commence ... I feel the warm spring waters running down my hair and over every inch of my body, draining away mental fatigue and restoring vibrant life ...

I now imagine the bright sunlight reaching deep within ... filtering out and washing away all my limiting and destructive attitudes, particularly my negative thoughts ...

Readjusting and turning off the Shower I now step out, instantly dry, and fresh with positive expectations ...

In a moment I will create my Boardroom, which is entered by a doorway off my Central Hallway ... I am now leaving my Conditioning Gym and entering my Central Hallway. The walls are covered with images depicting moments from my past when I have been at my very best ...

I am now creating the room that will house my Boardroom ... I am choosing the size of this area and the height of the ceiling ... Now I am choosing the decorative features, the colours and the lighting ... I am installing three comfortable chairs and a boardroom table of whatever size I choose ... I am now installing a full-length window with a door that opens onto my inner gardens and the landscape of abundance beyond ...

I will now leave the house and return to the river's edge ...

I feel the lush green grass beneath my feet. Soon I will count from 1 to 7, and gradually adjust to come out of this healthy state of deep relaxation ...

1 ... 2 ... 3 ... 4 ... now, beyond the midpoint, when I open my eyes I will be wide awake and revitalized both physically and mentally ... 5, I begin to adjust my body ... 6, I prepare to open my eyes ... and 7, I open my eyes and am wide awake now, both physically and mentally alert.

Using Your Board of Directors

You will gain the most from your Board of Directors if you are fully relaxed when you consult them, so it is always advisable to follow the Standard Entry Exercise first. However, as the previous exercise shows you can also use the tip-of-the-tongue trigger to enter your House on the Right Bank if you are short of time. Indeed, you can enter your house, use your Shower and enter your Boardroom in a couple of seconds if you need to consult your directors urgently. I often do this in meetings or when I am giving a course and am asked a question that I am unsure how to answer. I use the tip-of-the-tongue trigger, enter my Boardroom and ask my directors for advice. I listen to what they have to say, then use this information to form my own reply.

I have been using my Boardroom for many years, so I have collected quite a number of directors by now. In fact, I have seven permanent directors, and one who drops in from time to time. My first woman director was a very personal choice which I do not talk about, and the first male director I chose was Richard Branson because I admire him so much. Over the years I have added five other people I truly admire – Jesus Christ, Sir John Harvey Jones, Zig Zigler, Billy Connolly, and Anita Roddick. The director who drops in every now and then, when he's not too busy doing other things, is the actor Robin Williams. Between them my directors give me fantastic advice, and I love listening to them talk.

Making the Most of Your Sleep

As I told you in Chapter Five, the thoughts you have before you go to sleep are the most important ones of your whole day because they have the strongest effect on you. This is because you are thinking while your brain is in alpha/theta. If you use the MindStore techniques in this book you will never again go to sleep thinking negative thoughts such as, 'I'm dreading tomorrow,' 'I'll never get to sleep' or any other type of negative self-talk we have all indulged in from time to time. Instead you will go to sleep each night feeling relaxed and fully prepared for a wonderful night's sleep. You will also go to sleep knowing that, while your body catches up on vital rest and goes about its business of restoring and repairing itself, your subconscious mind will be busy working away on your behalf.

Edison's Pad

Have you ever used the phrase 'I'll sleep on it' when making a decision? And how many times did you wake in the morning with the calm certainty of one whose mind is made up and who knows exactly what to do? Sleeping on decisions and problems definitely works.

Thomas Edison, one of the greatest inventors of all time, regularly used to sleep on his problems. He even devised a special tool, which I call 'Edison's Pad', to enable him to make the most of his thoughts while he was asleep.

If you use it too you will be able to maximize your thought processes at the time when they are at their most creative.

To create your own Edison's Pad, all you need is a notepad and pen, which from now on you will always keep by your bed. Whenever you go away for a night or two, you will take the notepad with you.

- On the top sheet of the notepad, write clearly in block capitals: 'I AM ABOUT TO GO TO SLEEP AND I WILL FIND THE SOLUTION TO [the task/challenge you are facing].'
- Get into bed and enter your Sleeping Quarters by the Direct Access Route, using the tip-of-the-tongue trigger. Use the Shower in your Conditioning Gym, then enter your Sleeping Quarters, set your giant Opportunity Clock and follow the Pathway to Sleep. Instead of the usual repetition, state: 'I am falling into a deep, relaxing sleep and I will find a solution to [the task/challenge you are facing].'
- When you wake up, the solution will either appear in your conscious mind as a flash of insight, or it will have appeared in your subconscious mind during the night as a dream. Whichever way it arrives, write down the solution on your Edison's Pad so you can reflect on it later in the day.
- If you wake up in the morning and do not have or sense a solution, enter your House on the Right Bank by the Standard Entry Exercise, go into your Editing Suite and programme yourself finding the solution during the day. Mentally say to yourself: 'I am about to go into my day, and during the day I will find a solution to [the task/challenge you are facing].'

Dream On

The creative genius, Mozart, regularly used to wake up in the night hearing the orchestra in his head playing a beautiful, complete, piece of music. He would leap out of bed and write it all down, note for note, as he heard it. Our world is richer for his nocturnal compositions, but I sometimes wonder what would have happened if Mozart had woken up, heard the music and thought, 'Oh, I can't be bothered to write this down tonight. I'll do it tomorrow,' only to wake up the following morning unable to remember a single note! How many life-enhancing pieces of music would have been lost for ever?

It's not only Mozart who experienced powerful, creative ideas in the middle of the night. Throughout the centuries many writers, poets, artists and composers have woken up with their new work fully formed in their heads and rushed to get it down on paper. You can be exactly the same, because great ideas can come to everyone. You may have already missed quite a few of your own, especially if you have ever woken from a vivid dream, thought 'What a fantastic idea! I'll be sure to remember that in the morning,' then woken up at your usual time and found your great idea had completely vanished, or seemed to make no sense to the logical, left-hand side of your brain? Sometimes in the process of writing these things down, even if they seem to be 'illogical', you find that there is the germ of a great idea within the seemingly jumbled thoughts or images that come to you in the middle of the night.

Some of the world's cultures believe implicitly in the importance of dreams, with everyone in that culture allocating time each day to exploring the meaning and significance of their dreams. The Senoi people of the Malayan rain forest spend each morning analysing their dreams. They even hold dream councils, in which the adults in the tribe recount and analyse one another's dreams. They believe that everything that happens in dreams has a purpose, so they dedicate a lot of time to discovering what that purpose is. Perhaps the most amazing and persuasive advertisement for the value of the Senoi people's dream analyses is that they have not experienced a single case of violence or conflict in over 300 years. Wouldn't it be great if you could say the same thing about your neighbourhood?

Making a Dream Log

The next time you wake up having just had a very vivid dream, ask yourself this simple question: 'Why have I woken up to remember this dream?' If you believe, like the Senoi people, that dreams have a purpose, you will want to explore the message in your dreams. But don't trust that you will remember the dream in the morning, because the chances are that you won't. You must write down the details of your dream immediately, preferably in a Dream Log like the one shown below. *Then* you can go back to sleep!

I have to admit that logging your dreams takes a lot of willpower at first. You will have to rouse yourself from your comfortable position, switch on the light if necessary, sit up in bed, maybe put on your glasses, and then write down the details of your dream. But if you really want to maximize your thought processes and tap into your subconscious, you will soon find it is time well spent. Do it as soon as you wake up, whatever time it happens to be, and don't allow your logical, left brain to tell you it's nonsense or persuade you to wait until the morning, because your dream will have evaporated by then.

Never be tempted to analyse a dream in the middle of the night. Your right brain created the dream and will want you to know what it means, but your logical, left brain will tell you not to bother because it's the middle of the night, for goodness sake! So wait until the following day, and preferably the evening, before looking at your Dream Log and reading the details of the dream again. Now you are in a position to answer three very important questions:

1   Is the dream connected to the events that took place yesterday?
2   Is the dream connected to the events that took place today?
3   Is the dream connected to whatever else is going on in my life?

DESCRIPTION OF DREAM

| HOW DOES THE DREAM RELATE TO WHAT HAPPENED YESTERDAY? | HOW DOES IT RELATE TO WHAT HAPPENED TODAY? |

HOW DOES IT RELATE TO WHATEVER ELSE IS GOING ON IN YOUR LIFE?

A Dream Log

Think carefully before writing down your answers to each of these questions. Remember, it's not a test and no one else is going to read this Dream Log, so feel free to express your thoughts. If you suspect that a dream is related to a particular part of your life but aren't sure, then say so. You may even find that, although a dream doesn't appear to make much sense on the Thursday night that you dreamed it, by the following Wednesday its meaning will be as clear as day.

To create your own Dream Log all you need is a large sheet of paper and access to a photocopier. Copy the Dream

Log shown above on to the paper, then make as many photo-copies of it as you can. Keep it on your bedside table, with a pen, and always take it with you when you spend a night away from home.

If you do not usually remember your dreams, you can programme yourself to do so:

- On the top sheet of a notepad, write clearly in block capitals: 'I AM ABOUT TO GO TO SLEEP AND DREAM, AND ON AWAKENING I WILL REMEMBER A DREAM.'
- Get into bed and enter your Sleeping Quarters by the Direct Access Route, using the tip-of-the-tongue trigger. Use the Shower in your Conditioning Gym, then enter your Sleeping Quarters, set your giant Opportunity Clock and follow the Pathway to Sleep. Instead of the usual repetition, state: 'I am about to go to sleep and dream, and on awakening I will remember a dream.'
- When you wake up it is very important that you write down the details of your dream immediately so you can reflect on it later in the day.

The more you practise recording and analysing your dreams, the more they will tell you, and the more in tune you will become with your intuition. Try it, and remember – *it only works*.

7

The Tip-of-the-Tongue Trigger

In this chapter I want to talk about a tool that I have already mentioned several times: the tip-of-the-tongue trigger, which provides an instant way of entering your House on the Right Bank.

Of course, it is always most effective to enter your house using the Standard Entry Exercise – in other words, to relax your body completely, then visit your favourite place of relaxation before altering your focus to your landscape of abundance. However, there are times when you will need instant access to your House on the Right Bank, and I call this the Direct Access Route. All you do is gently curl up your tongue and place the tip of it on the roof of your mouth directly behind your two front teeth. Tests using electro-encephalograms have proved that this simple manoeuvre automatically puts your brain into alpha/theta.

Putting My Finger On the Trigger

When I was putting together the MindStore course, which was several years ago now, I knew that I needed to create a technique that would instantly switch my brain into alpha/theta, but I could not find a solution anywhere. Finally I realized that I would have to use my Edison's Pad to find the answer, so before going to sleep one night I programmed myself to discover the solution by the time I woke up in the morning. In the middle of the night I woke up and, as usual, went along to the bathroom to relieve myself. I was disappointed that the solution I had programmed had not yet come to me, but I knew I still had several hours' more sleep in which to find it.

The house we lived in at that time had a bookcase on the landing, just beside the bathroom door. As I walked out of the bathroom I found myself looking intently at one of the bookshelves. 'Why on earth am I looking at these bookshelves?' I wondered. 'What's so special about them?' When I thought this, I realized I was looking at one book in particular, so I took it off the shelf and studied it. The book I had chosen was one I had not opened in years. In fact, I was surprised to see I still owned it, because I had never read it. It was a yellowing, rather stained book on yoga that I had bought from a second-hand bookshop years before, when I was trying to impress a girl I knew who was interested in yoga. My ruse had failed but I had kept the book, despite never bothering to look at it again. But now I turned it over in my hands a couple of times, then opened it at random and started to read.

There, in black and white, was the solution I had programmed myself to find. The book said that many practitioners of yoga use a technique that enables them to slow down their brain waves and concentrate more deeply on their yoga. All they do is to place the tip of their tongue on the roof of their mouth directly behind their two front teeth. By the way, I have since discovered that T'ai Chi employs the same technique.

I was amazed, but I was also keen to check that what the yoga book said was true, so I had myself wired up to an electro-encephalogram at Stirling University. That's how I know for certain that deep relaxation changes your brain waves from beta to alpha or theta, and that's also how I know that the tip-of-the-tongue trigger does the same thing. It acts like an on-off switch between beta and alpha/theta brain waves. It's been used for all these centuries – why should I have doubted it? Once you have established the anchor (as in the exercise featured on page 93), you can continue to practise the technique each time you visit your House on the Right Bank, to build trust in it.

Using the Tip-of-the-Tongue Trigger

I have already mentioned several specific uses for the tip-of-the-tongue trigger in the previous chapters. These include:

- improving your concentration and performance in meetings and your recall of them afterwards
- improving your ability to listen to what other people are saying
- reading in your Library of Knowledge and remembering what you have read
- recalling information, consulting your teacher or visiting your Library of Knowledge during an exam
- breaking habits such as smoking, over-eating and procrastinating

- making quick decisions
- consulting your Board of Directors
- programming yourself to dream or to think of a solution to a problem as you sleep.

I am sure you will find your own ways of using the tip-of-the-tongue trigger as well. Remember, it is most effective if you keep your tongue in position throughout the time you are visiting your House on the Right Bank if you have entered it through the Direct Access Route. You can also keep your tongue in position when you visit your house using the Standard Entry Exercise, as this will act as an anchor and strengthen the quality of your alpha/theta brain waves.

Programming Parking Spaces

This is something that always proves very popular with MindStore members. I have lost count of the number of people who bump into me in the street, in shops, on trains and on planes, and tell me that, with the help of this tool, they have become champion car-parkers.

This tool is particularly useful on Saturday mornings when the rain is bucketing down and you've got to go shopping. Instead of driving around for hours looking in vain for a parking space, you will be able to programme being able to park right outside the shop you want to visit. Here's what you do:

- Get in your car but, before you turn on the ignition, close your eyes and use the tip-of-the-tongue trigger. Mentally rehearse parking your car exactly where you would like to be able to park it.

- Start your car and drive off as normal. Sure enough, your parking space will be waiting for you.

As with all the other techniques in this book, you must have the desire to achieve your goal, otherwise you will not be successful.

Programming Taxis

You can use this tool for programming taxis, which are also something that are in short supply on rainy Saturday mornings. However, I would urge you to be very specific when you do this. Only recently my team and I were walking along a London street, looking for a taxi that would take us off to a restaurant for dinner. I had programmed that a taxi would come along before we reached the end of the road, and sure enough it did, but I had forgotten to programme that it would be empty. As a result, it already had a passenger and it drove straight past us!

You can have a lot of fun programming taxis. If you're feeling chatty, programme one with a talkative driver. If it's one of those days when you'd rather be left alone, make sure you programme a driver who barely speaks a word.

This tool will work just as well if you want to programme an empty table at a busy restaurant, a seat on the bus or train on the way home, a quiet person next to you at the theatre or cinema, and so on. These are all fun ways of using the tip-of-the-tongue trigger and they can work phenomenally well, but please use it too for the more serious techniques in this book. After all, if it works well for securing you a parking space, think how well it will work for improving your relationships or helping you to lose weight.

Improving Your Game

The tip-of-the-tongue trigger is invaluable when it comes to improving your performance at sport. All the great sports-people now use mental rehearsals to improve their techniques and practise winning. Remember Muhammad Ali and his future histories? You can do the same.

In my House on the Right Bank, I have a bowling green. It is part of my inner garden. When I first created it, it would not be indulging in false modesty to say I was an average bowls player. I belonged to a local bowls club, but I knew my fellow-members would never count on me to beat the other clubs hands down. However, I started to practise in my imagination on my bowling green. And inside six weeks I was playing for my county. *It only works!*

The tip-of-the-tongue trigger also works wonderfully for golfers. Not long ago I went to Belfast to do a MindStore course, and got talking to a guy who plays golf. He told me excitedly that he had doubled his income and halved his handicap at golf. I asked him about the golf – what was he doing that made such a fantastic difference? (I was hoping I might pick up a few tips.) He told me that he mentally rehearses each shot using the tip-of-the-tongue trigger, then he pulls the club back and, just before he strikes the ball, he says to himself 'OK, Seve, take over.'

Creating Other Rooms

Recently, a MindStore member told me she enjoys doing competitions, so she created a special room in her House on the Right Bank in which to do them. She goes in there using the Standard Entry Exercise and also the tip-of-the-tongue trigger. Then, when she is nicely relaxed, she does her competitions and, sure enough, she's winning everything in sight.

I hope you will create more rooms in your house in which you can do all the things you are interested in. Many artists have told me they have created studios in which they mentally produce their works of art, down to the last detail, before making the real thing. Musicians, writers, sculptors, dress-makers and other creative people also use these techniques, and report that they work in phenomenal ways.

Next time you have to cook a special meal, why not create your own state-of-the-art kitchen in your House on the Right Bank and use the tip-of-the-tongue trigger to rehearse the whole procedure, finishing with sighs of contentment from your satisfied and replete guests. You could even make one of the people on your Board of Directors a cook whom you truly admire, then ask him or her to come and help you in your kitchen. The delicious results will speak for themselves.

If you pride yourself on looking well-groomed, you could choose a hairdresser or make-up artist as one of your Directors, then consult his or her advice every morning. The possibilities are endless – so have fun discovering how far your imagination will take you.

8

Food for Thought

If, as the saying goes, we are what we eat, what does that make you? Does it mean you are as healthy and full of vitality as the fresh fruit and vegetables you eat every day, or does it mean that too often you are full of junk food, chocolate and ready-prepared meals?

In this chapter I want to talk about the importance of food in your life. As I said earlier, computer programmers have a phrase – GIGO, or 'garbage in, garbage out'. For them, this refers to the idea that a computer is only as good as the information that is fed into it. Well, the same is true of our bodies. Even though they are far more sophisticated than any computer, and have a much higher tolerance level for garbage, there comes a time when our bodies start to malfunction if they do not get the nutrients and treatment they require. Most often there won't be a sudden or dramatic change in your body. Instead, it's very gradual. You start to feel more tired more often, you begin to suffer from indigestion, you catch more than your fair share of colds, your skin becomes pasty or you feel sluggish and out of sorts. These are all very common health problems and you may resign yourself to having to live with them, yet you don't have to.

Eating to Live

Do you live to eat or do you eat to live? Many people definitely do the former, and it can have very challenging effects on their waistlines as well as their health. It is very easy to regard food as a great solace and comfort, especially on those days when nothing goes right. You could feel a lot happier, so you cheer yourself up with a cup of coffee and a bar of chocolate, or treat yourself to a big pile of chips at lunch time. If you haven't got time for a proper lunch-break you have a bag of crisps and a fizzy drink at your desk while you carry on working. But after an hour or so you start to feel sleepy and lethargic, so you have another cup of coffee or fizzy drink to wake yourself up, and so it goes on.

If any of this sounds familiar, then I can assure you that you're not alone. But what can you do about it?

The first alteration you need to make in your life is the way you think about food. Once you regard it as the vital fuel that your body needs to function properly every day, your attitude towards food will start to change. After all, how can you expect your body to operate in peak condition if you are giving it inferior food, such as highly processed meals, a sugary snack instead of a lunch-time sandwich, and lots of fatty fast foods? An oil-fired central heating boiler, for example, will instantly become nothing more than a pile of scrap metal if you decide to feed it lemonade one day because you've run out of oil. So if you are feeling less than great, maybe it's because you aren't giving your body the food it needs. And maybe it's also because you are eating at the wrong times of day for your body.

The Body Clock

Medical and scientific research has proved that the human body operates in cycles. There is the sleep cycle, which ensures we receive a good, long sleep every night, and there is also the food cycle, which ensures that our bodies carry out certain functions at certain times of the day. Researchers have discovered that the body has three cycles connected with food, each one of which is roughly eight hours long:

4 a.m. – noon	The body rids itself of all the waste products and toxins it has accumulated in the past 24 hours. Your body needs freedom from food during this time.
Noon – 8 p.m.	The body is ready to take in food. The ideal time to eat.
8 p.m. – 4 a.m.	The body uses and processes the food it has taken in during the previous cycle. This is when the body converts food into the vital fuel it needs to repair itself, rebuild cells, and so on.

What's for Breakfast?

Do you remember, in the 1960s, being told to 'go to work on an egg'? For decades it was generally believed that breakfast was a very important meal because it would set us up for the day ahead. We were all encouraged to eat a good, hearty breakfast, and most of us did. But how did we feel halfway through the morning? Unless we were doing heavy manual work, a lot of us felt listless and certainly *not* the way we had been promised we would feel.

If you have always followed the advice to eat a good breakfast and wouldn't dream of starting the day in any other way, then I have news for you: The latest research indicates that our bodies are *not* designed to cope with a big meal first thing we wake up. As the body cycles printed above show, at breakfast time the body is busy getting rid of waste products. It does not have much energy to spare for digestion. If you eat breakfast, your body will reluctantly process your food very, very slowly and you will not get a great deal of nourishment from it.

For many people the answer is to eat fresh fruit for breakfast, especially if they spend most of the day using their brains rather than their brawn. Fresh fruit only stays in the stomach for about 15 minutes before being passed into the small intestine, where it is broken down immediately into fructose, a natural form of sugar. This is absorbed into the walls of the small intestine and, from there, is slowly released into the bloodstream as the body needs it. The result is tremendous clarity of thought (vital if you want to use your creative right brain), no hunger pangs, and bags of energy. If you feel a little peckish halfway through the morning, you simply have some more fruit.

As with all rules, there are some exceptions. If you will be spending the day in strenuous activity, you need to eat a bigger breakfast full of carbohydrates because you will be using up so much energy. Women may find that they need a carbohydrate breakfast at certain times of the month. It is all a question of listening to what your body tells you. However, if you have a breakfast of fresh fruit for ten days, I suspect that the difference it makes to your day – and to the quality of your thoughts – will be so great that you will never go back to your old breakfast. I breakfast on fresh fruit every working day and I love it, though I sometimes have porridge if I'm on holiday.

Food Combining

If you start to eat fresh fruit for breakfast and love the way it clarifies your thoughts and fills you with energy, you might like to take things one step further and explore the fascinating idea of food combining. This is also known as the Hay diet, after Dr William Hay, who developed the idea at the turn of the century.

Food combining is a very simple system of eating that allows your body to derive the maximum nourishment and benefit from your food. It is based on the idea that foods can be divided into three categories – starchy foods, proteins and neutral foods. Neutral foods (such as vegetables and fats) mix happily with either starches or proteins. Starches and proteins do not mix well with each other at all, because the stomach digests each of them in a different way. The stomach uses acids to break down protein foods, and alkalines to digest carbohydrates. Now, you will remember from school that one of the basic laws of chemistry says that mixing acids and alkalines together neutralizes them. So if you eat a meal consisting of starch and protein, such as a baked potato (starch) topped with grated cheese (protein), your stomach's alkaline and acid digestive juices will cancel each other out. The result is that the food will stay in your stomach for a long time because it will have difficulty digesting these different types of food. Also, you won't absorb all the food's goodness. And that's not a very efficient way of eating, is it?

Food-combiners derive the maximum goodness from their food because they eat it in the right combinations. It is estimated that a meal consisting of vegetables and carbohydrates or vegetables and proteins will be processed by the stomach efficiently in three or four hours, whereas a meal of mixed proteins and carbohydrates may take a lot longer. The food combining ideal is to have one neutral meal (which is where the fruit breakfast comes in), one starch meal, and one protein meal each day. You should eat plenty of vegetables, preferably in the form of salads, with the protein and starch meals.

Food combining has many benefits. Many chronic medical conditions, from Irritable Bowel Syndrome to arthritis, have been cured by food combining because it allows your body to process food in the way that nature intended. Thousands of years ago, when human beings were hunter-gatherers, they ate one food at a time – a wild animal, some berries, some vegetables or whatever else they found. They certainly didn't think 'I'll pick some fresh young nettles to go with this wild boar, and then we'll have some lovely wild strawberries for pudding.' Life wasn't like that – you ate your food as and when you found it.

In Dr Hay's view, the five most important foods for the body, in this order, are:

1   fruit
2   salads and leafy green vegetables
3   root vegetables
4   grains
5   proteins.

With the accent on fresh fruit, vegetables and wholefood products, you get a balanced, healthy range of foods. You may also find that you effortlessly lose that spare tyre around your waist, or that double chin, because you have changed the balance of the foods you eat and therefore the number of calories you eat each day. Instead of eating a lot of fats and proteins, of which your body only needs a little, you replace them with plenty of fresh fruit, vegetables and complex carbohydrates. You will also learn to eat when you are hungry, instead of when the clock tells you to.

There are some excellent books available on food combining, and I have listed some of the best ones in the Further Information chapter at the back of this book. Food combining is particularly suitable for vegetarians because of its emphasis on fresh fruit and vegetables, but it is just as good for meat-eaters. Why not try food combining for a couple of weeks, just taking it gently at first, and see how you feel? I think you will be pleasantly surprised at the difference in your levels of energy and vitality.

Food combining is powerful stuff. It works very well for me, because it gives me the bags of physical energy I need to run courses from nine in the morning till late at night if needs be. It also helps me to keep my weight in check. I don't always follow it rigidly, especially when I am on holiday, but I have found it invaluable. If you are interested in nutrition and getting the maximum benefit from your food, I can really recommend food combining. By the way, don't be misled by the name 'the Hay diet'. This is not a gimmicky diet that you follow for a couple of weeks – it is a way of eating that will become a way of life.

Allergies

Food combiners say that many apparent allergies to certain foods disappear when you follow the Hay diet. It often turns out that you were allergic to the combination of certain foods, and not the foods themselves. For instance, cheese sandwiches may leave you doubled up with indigestion, so you think you are allergic to cheese, but when you start to food-combine you may find that you can eat cheese in a protein meal with no after-effects at all. It was the mixture of bread and cheese that caused the indigestion.

However, there is a simple kinaesthetic way to test if you are allergic to anything – you don't have to wait for your stomach or skin to tell you. You can use this method to discover if you are allergic to metals, types of clothing, particular cosmetics, bath products and so on. All you need is a willing helper.

The test is very similar to one that I do in the MindStore courses, when I prove that thoughts can affect our physical strength. If you have not yet attended one of the courses (and I am looking forward to welcoming you to one soon), let me describe what happens. I ask for two male volunteers from the audience – this is because the results are more startling when they affect strong-looking men – then I test their strength. I ask each one to hold out his right arm (if he is right-handed), then I push down on it with all my might. The guy's arm always resists my strength, and I have shown the audience how strong he is. Then I ask the guy to think of something negative, and I try the arm-test again. This time, without fail, the guy finds to his astonishment that he has lost all strength in his arm. The negative thought has affected his body in a physical way, and proves how important it is to think positively. I then repeat the test by asking the man to put a cigarette in his mouth. Again he has no strength.

You can conduct this same kinaesthetic test with various foods and objects. You can do it either by holding the object in front of you and asking your willing helper to test your arm's strength, or you can ask him or her to stand behind you and hold the object at the back of your neck. Amazingly enough, your body will still register what the object is and you will react according to whether you are compatible with it or not. This second method also ensures that your conscious thoughts do not affect the outcome, as they might do if the object or food is facing you.

Nutritionists use this simple test to discover what their clients are allergic to, and I would urge you to try it at home. You will be astonished at the results, and may also find that they make a lot of sense. For instance, let's say you've never liked Brussels sprouts and think they upset your stomach. Sure enough, the arm test shows that you are allergic to them.

I am delighted to tell you that, although many alcoholic drinks do not come out well from this arm test (especially low-alcohol lagers, which are full of chemicals), malt whisky is fine for me! However, do try it for yourself, because what suits one person does not always suit another.

Creative Drinking

Talking of malt whisky brings me to another subject that is very dear to my heart, but for different reasons – coffee. People who attend my MindStore courses soon discover this for themselves, because after the mid-morning break on the first day no more tea or coffee is served. There is plenty of water, but tea and coffee are banned! That is because both interfere with your creative right brain, although coffee presents by far the strongest challenge.

If someone tests you for coffee, whether it is cheap, instant granules, decaffeinated coffee or the expensive, freshly ground stuff, you will find you have no strength in your arm. Coffee (which, incidentally, is the second biggest industry in the world, after oil) does not do your body any favours at all. As we all know, it is a stimulant, and the moment you swallow it you experience a powerful charge because it produces high beta frequencies in the brain. It feels great, and I should know because I used to drink 14 or 15 cups of the stuff every day – I was a true coffeeholic. However, the kick that you get from coffee comes at a price – high beta frequencies stop the low frequencies of your right brain working. So, if you drink coffee all day long you will *never* be able to use the House on the Right Bank properly. You may also find it hard to sleep, because the alpha and theta frequencies will be blocked by the beta waves.

I know that if you've been drinking a lot of coffee day in, day out, you will experience real withdrawal symptoms when you stop. But headaches and lethargy are simply the effects of your body ridding itself of all those toxins. In fact, instead of thinking how terrible you feel and that you'd better go back to drinking coffee because you obviously need it, tell yourself that you obviously need to give it up because of the way its poisons have accumulated in your body. Once you stop drinking coffee you will never want to return to it, because the difference in your well-being will be amazing.

As I have said, tea presents less of a challenge; it's up to you to see how it affects you. If you can't bear the thought of giving up coffee *and* tea, treat yourself to some good-quality teas such as Darjeeling, Earl Grey and Chinese green tea. They contain less caffeine and tannin than cheaper teas. You can also drink fruit teas and herbal teas, both of which are very good for you.

If you value your health and your creative abilities, please make sure you avoid sweet, fizzy drinks. Many of them are packed with caffeine and will produce high beta frequencies. They are also full of sugar, drain you of energy, and don't do you any good at all. They, as well as coffee, are not allowed in our MindStore offices because I feel so strongly about them.

As I write this I am beginning to experiment with a macrobiotic diet as a means of counteracting the effects of continual travel and eating in restaurants and hotels. In doing so I am looking for even greater benefits for my health and energy. You might be interested in trying this for yourself, or experimenting with food combining. But whatever you choose to eat, enjoy your food and chew it well, much more than you do at the moment, so your body can digest it properly and gain the maximum nutrition from it.

Finally, as the chapter heading says, all this is food for thought. Food combining isn't an essential ingredient of the MindStore techniques, but I have found that it has made me feel so fit, well and energetic that I think you will benefit from it as well. And if you really want to become more creative, you will soon discover the difference that cutting out coffee makes. The choice is, of course, yours, but I am sure that once you begin to discover the benefits and rewards of the MindStore techniques contained in this book, you will want to stay healthy so you can enjoy as many of them as possible.

Keep smiling!

Recommended Reading List

Mindstore by Jack Black (Thorsons, 1994)
The Inner Game of Golf by Timothy Galwey (Pan, 1986)
The Inner Game of Tennis by Timothy Galwey (Pan, 1986)
Drawing on the Right Side of the Brain by Betty Edwards
    (HarperCollins, 1993)
The Celestine Prophecy by James Redfield (Bantam, 1994)
The Celestine Prophecy: An Experiential Guide by James
    Redfield and Carol Adrienne (Bantam, 1995)
Think and Grow Rich by Napoleon Hill
    (HarperCollins, 1970)
Success Through a Positive Mental Attitude by Napoleon
    Hill and W Clement Stone (Thorsons, 1990)
The Magic of Thinking Big by David Schwartz
    (Pocket Books, 1995)
The Power of Your Subconscious Mind by Joseph Murphy
    (Pocket Books, 1995)
Use Your Head by Tony Buzan (BBC Books, 1974)
Being Happy by Andrew Matthews (Media Masters, 1987)

Food Combining for Health by Doris Grant and Jean Joice
(Thorsons, 1984)
Food Combining for Vegetarians by Jackie Le Tissier
(Thorsons, 1993)
The Food Combining Diet by Kathryn Marsden
(Thorsons 1993)

Most of the above books are available through MindStore.

At the time of writing, all these books are in print. If you have difficulty in obtaining them at your local library or bookshop, MindStore operates a mail-order service for many of these titles. For more information about the books available from MindStore, or if you would like details of the MindStore courses and/or cassette tapes for the business community, the general public, and children, please contact:

MindStore
MindStore House
36 Speirs Wharf
Port Dundas
Glasgow G4 9TB
Tel: 0141–333 9393

Index